The Crappiest Year Ever

Keith Nimz

Copyright © 2012 Keith Nimz

All rights reserved.

ISBN:1480009113
ISBN-13: 9781480009110

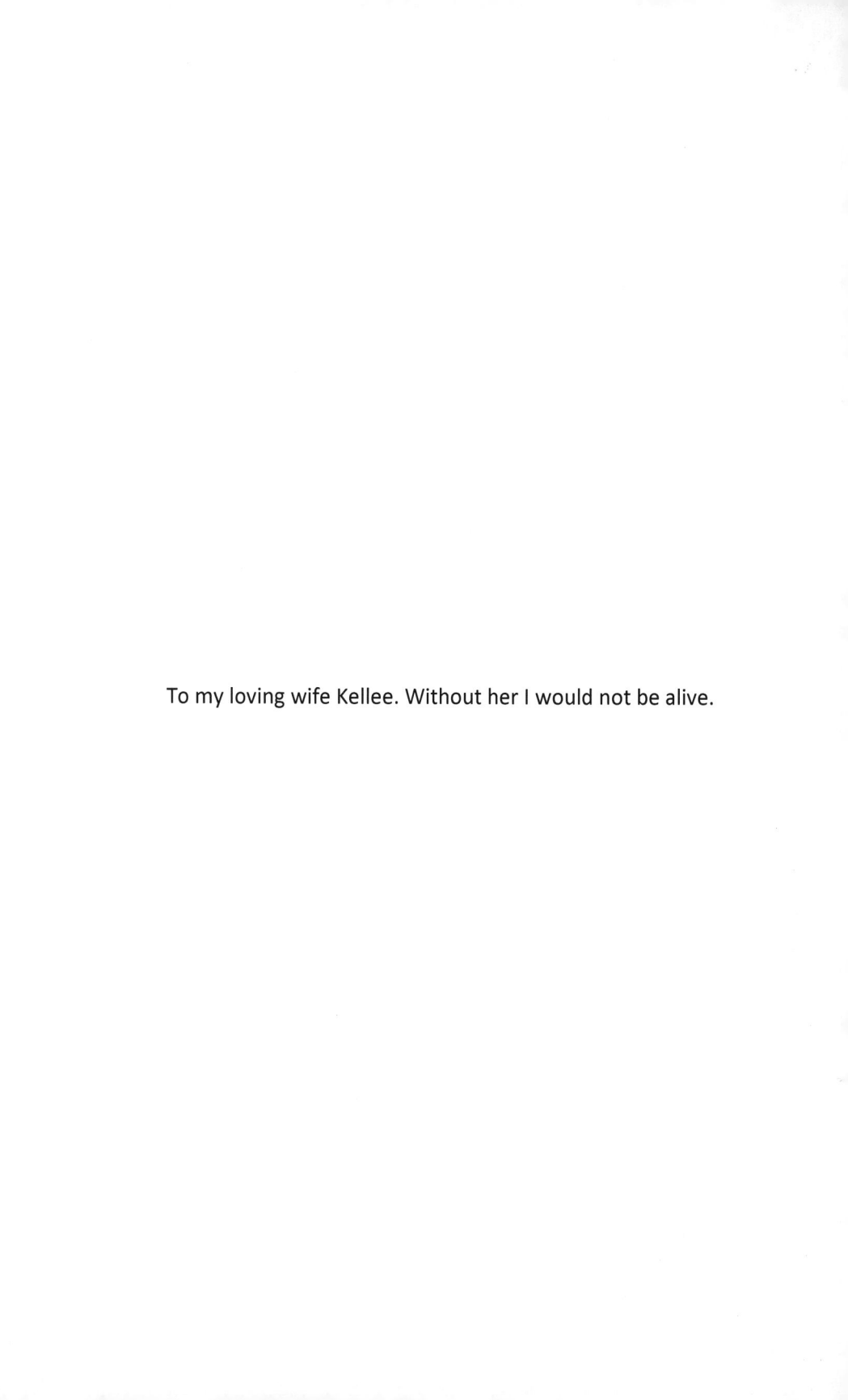

To my loving wife Kellee. Without her I would not be alive.

CONTENTS

	Acknowledgments	i
1	In The Beginning	1
2	A fallen Hero	4
3	Clinging To Life	8
4	Receiving Life	13
5	Discovering The Truth	16
6	Losing Hope	21
7	Going Under The Knife	24
8	I'm In Hell	30
9	Past Revisited	34
10	First Steps	38
11	A Room With A View	41
12	Balloon Day	44
13	I Can See Clearly Now	46
14	A Feast Fit For A King	48
15	Healing	53
16	Going Home	55
17	Home At Last	58
18	Day One	62
19	On The Road Again	64

20	Wedding Bells	68
21	Emergency Room	71
22	The Port	76
23	Chemotherapy	80
24	Precursor	87
25	An Angel Is Dying	90
26	An Angel Is Dying Part II	95
27	Death Of An Angel	104
28	Ease His Pain	109
29	The Truth	112
30	Support	114
31	Never Alone	118
32	Heaven	120
33	Struggling	124
34	Storms On The Horizon	127
35	The Big One	131
36	Home Away From Home	136
37	Dinner With A Side Of Hit And Run	141
38	Down To The Last Minute	145
39	It's A Wonderful Life	151
40	It's Over. Or Is It?	154

In loving memory of my mother, Doris Nimz.

You gave me life, you nurtured it, and you helped me become the man I am today. I love you and miss you dearly.

Special Thanks To:

Larry and Doris Nimz

My aunt Stephanie Nimz Boness,

Your support meant a lot.

Stephen and Carol Mastroianni

Marcy Holland

With out your help none of this would have been possible.

Jesse Mrugalski

We should all be so lucky to have your courage and spirit.

www.bimmerforums.com

Sachin

Sneezy: Jack

mz.368: Jen

Sparkchaser: Rob (Hipster)

M Shareef

Guarddog: Patrick A

RocketWagon: Stephen

Keith Nimz

Special Thanks To:

Cajun: Shane

M3blurr: Barney

Triggrhaapi: Jason

EightGodzillas: Shane

Slvr328is: Paolo

Dryle: Dave

Dane Wilson77: Dane

Ladiexmack: Mackenzie

Lockdots: Miguel

HD7: Jason (SuperJay)

Kevlar: Kevin

www.zhpmafia.com

Cakm3: Charlie

Marcus-SanDiego: Mark

Chapter 1

In The Beginning

Life has never been easy for me. No matter how simple something was supposed to be, it always turned into a huge fiasco. As a child going to school I didn't simply wake up, gather my things and go. My mornings consisted of me carefully choosing my meals, mentally prepping myself for the worst, and downing awful medicine with hopes that it would keep my stomach calm long enough to make it through the day. I was diagnosed with Irritable Bowel Syndrome at a young age. Any time I was stressed or if I ate the wrong foods, my body's digestive tract protested in painful, embarrassing, and even stressful ways. I felt trapped. I couldn't go anywhere or do anything without having to worry about whether or not my stomach would cooperate.

It wasn't all just about the IBS though. Looking back at my life I think I was too smart for my own good when I was young. At times when other kids my age only cared about their favorite cartoons, or playing baseball, I was worried about the world, my future, people, everything. I over analyzed the world around me. No matter the situation, every encounter and interaction buzzed through my head to the point that I broke down every last moment and studied it until it was meaningless. This often separated me from the rest of the world and brought stress on me that someone shouldn't have growing up.

Much like any young person, I too suffered from "teenage angst" when growing up. Couple that with my over analytical brain and lifelong illness of Irritable Bowel Syndrome - I felt like a complete outcast. I was alone in the world and lived a pretty solitary life and fought depression through most of high school. Sure I had friends, but for the most part I still felt very alone. I drifted through school doing what I could to make it to the end of each day, praying that my IBS would leave me alone for once.

I found myself falling in a downward spiral - lost with no way out. It's this feeling of helplessness that unfortunately causes a lot of young people to result to suicide. Often times they will feel like there is no other alternative, there's no reason to keep on living if life will always be that way. I believe that if I did not get my strength from my parents, I too would have succumbed to depression and would have chosen the dark path by ending my life a long time ago. I was fortunate that my parents taught me early on in life to be independent and to take care of myself. I learned to cook for myself, wash my own clothes, to be self-reliant when I needed to be. It wasn't that my parents didn't take care of me, far from it. They had raised three sons prior to me and had learned with each of them how to groom the next one. This has enabled me to take the hardships in stride and become an even stronger person. It wasn't easy, it never is, but the point was that I never gave up.

A few years after I had graduated high school, I found myself looking back on my life and the person I had become. I thought back to all the bad moments in life, all the times I felt like an outcast among my peers, and how horrible it made me feel. It was then that I realized that I had been looking at life the wrong way. I had spent my entire life focusing on all the bad things that happened to me and it just made me feel worse. I was wallowing in my own self-pity and never realized it.

Sure I had been through a lot of bad things, who hasn't? I pulled through it though. I did manage to find happiness in between all the hardships. I soon found that if I focused more on the positive aspects of my life like the things I were grateful for and lucky to have, life suddenly didn't seem all that bad.

Changing the way I thought turned my life around. I no longer felt like the weight of the world was crushing down on me. Instead of feeling alone and shying away from everyone, I found myself going out all the time with my friends and just enjoying every moment of it. I had never been happier in my life, and for the first time ever I felt like I could take on anything.

Little did I know that during the year of 2011, when I was only 29 years old, I would be put to the ultimate test. I would be pushed to my limits and beyond. The events that were about to unfold would change my view of the world forever, and I would never look at my life the same again. I learned how compassionate people can really be, even when they are total strangers. And when faced with my own mortality, I learned more about myself than I had ever known before. I was about to go through the worst part of my life, with no positive outlook on the horizon and no idea if I would be able to come out of it and be able to find happiness again.

Keith Nimz

Chapter 2

A Fallen Hero

Towards the end of 2010, my grandfather's health started slowly deteriorating, and it was expected that he might pass away soon. Eventually his condition was so bad that he was admitted to the hospital. After what had seemed like an eternity, his condition suddenly improved and it looked as though he might pull through. We had high hopes that perhaps he would be fine and live for another few years. Unfortunately, very quickly after his health improved, it took a turn for the worse and he passed away.

I have had a few friends pass away over the years so I knew the pain of losing someone, but I didn't know just how bad it would feel when it was a family member. Nothing could have prepared me for losing someone I had known my whole life and loved dearly. I remember just how lost I felt when I received the news of his passing. It felt like a giant stone had dropped from my chest to my stomach and made me feel sicker than I could imagine. I was lost. I wondered why, why him, why does such an amazing person have to be lost to this world?

My first instinct when hearing of his passing was to pack my clothes into my car right away and make the 500 mile trek to be there for his funeral. However, heartbreakingly, I could not. Mother Nature was against me and put a giant snow storm in my way which made travel impossible. The pain of losing him was even worse now because I could not be there to say a final goodbye to my grandfather.

Knowing that I could not be there for my mother and grandmother, I did what I could and sent flowers and called them on the phone to try to ease their pain. Of course with my bad luck, one of the bouquets of flowers ended up arriving dead and in shambles. Thankfully, with the help of my family, a replacement package was put together and finally made it to its destination. It accomplished what I had hoped for - it put a smile on both of their faces, even if just for a moment.

Years ago, my grandfather had heart surgery to have his failing valves replaced. The surgery was a success, but the doctors warned him that it was only a temporary solution. The new valves usually only last three to five years at most, and when they did fail he would again face surgery or even death. Though they only expected a few short years, his valves lasted him almost eight years. He was living on borrowed time, and for that I am grateful. If it wasn't for that extra time, he would have never met my wife and she would have missed out on meeting a real hero - a true inspiration of what people in this world should be like.

He was a loving father and grandfather. He was from a generation that I fear will never exist again. There was no quit in the man. He worked every day outside in his garden no matter how sick he was. He also faithfully took care of his wife whose health was also in question from time to time. Despite whatever obstacles were put in his way, he never gave in. He fought to the very end.

I have many memories of my grandfather from over the years and I'm lucky to say that all of them are good. There have always been two that stand out above all of them. Two that make me smile, and make me proud of him and love him dearly.

I always knew that when I was headed to Grandma and Grandpa's home, he would always have a box of soft chocolate chip cookies ready and waiting for me and my brother. After we would arrive and settled in, he would always give my brother and me two cookies each. Then he would break out the big box of Lego's for us to play with and we would spend the rest of the evening building and destroying our creations.

A few years later, I learned that my grandfather had served in the Navy during World War II. I remember staring in amazement at the plaques that hung on his wall that he earned from taking down enemy planes and boats. Before I knew of them, he just seemed like any other grandfather - a sweet old man who made you laugh and was fun to be around. Now, however, I had seen him in a whole new light. He had done the kind of things I only ever saw in movies or read about in books. That made him special. To me he was tougher and braver then all the other kids' grandfathers. It's simple fond memories like these which bring a smile to my face and make the loss of him easier.

I know that he would not want me to be sad about his passing. The sadness from missing him has gradually been replaced with happy memories of the time I spent with him, remembering his smile, his raspy laugh and how kind he was. I choose to remember how he lived rather than how he died, and it helps ease the sorrow of losing such a great man. It's not an easy task, and to this day I still get choked up at the thought of his passing, but by concentrating on the memories we made together it soon turns my sadness into happiness.

Starting with the passing of my grandfather, fate seemed to be taking a dislike for my family and me. I am telling the story of how this has been the worst year of my life, but in reality it has been the worst year of my family's life. It almost seems as if fate, or a higher power, maybe even the universe, had some kind of grievance with my family and decided to strike us down one after another in some way or form.

Right after my grandfather had passed away, my grandmother took a nasty fall and ended up in the hospital. Having just lost my grandfather, it instantly put fears in my head that I might lose her too. To our relief, she managed to recover and after a short stay at the hospital she was released. I remember how relieved I felt when I was told she was going home. The pain of losing my grandfather was still very fresh in all of our minds and the last thing any of us wanted, was to deal with it all over again.

Although my grandmother had escaped fate's grasp, it soon laid its eyes on my mother as her health began to deteriorate. Over the past ten years or so, she beat cancer on three separate occasions and now once again her health and her life were in jeopardy.

She started to have trouble breathing one evening, and thinking she would go to the doctor in the morning she ignored it and went to bed. During the night her condition worsened and she woke suddenly to find herself struggling to catch her breath. She woke my father, and he rushed her to the hospital for what was to be one of many visits over the next few months.

After the doctors examined her they found fluid in her lungs which was causing her to slowly suffocate. They removed the fluid and put her on medication to help prevent this from happening again. At the time we had no idea that this would be a precursor for what was to come and just how much she would suffer in the coming months.

Chapter 3

Clinging To Life

I spent the summer and early fall of 2010 hiking as much as possible. I would go out every week and hit the local trails in an effort to become healthier while seeing the sights. Every Monday morning I would pack up supplies and head out for one of two trails that I had grown to love. One was a short but scenic trail that followed a waterfall up the side of a mountain. The other was a more strenuous hike up to the top of a mountain which provided a breathtaking full circle view of the area. According to the trail maps, on a clear day you can see as far as Vermont which in itself is amazing since the mountain is located on the southern border of Massachusetts.

Come late fall it began to get too cold to hike anymore so I called it quits for the season with plans to pick it back up again next spring. I was feeling good; I had more stamina and was happy with the results. I had not been that fit in a long time. Prior to this I had not been regularly hiking for close to five years. When I lived in Pennsylvania, my friend, Bill, and I used to walk the local trails all the time. As long as it wasn't raining or snowing (sometimes that didn't even stop us) we were out there exploring.

As winter set in we happened to have one of the snowiest seasons we'd had in a long time. We endured snow storm after snow storm every week, each one dumping several feet on the ground. One of my duties at work is shoveling the snow, which always results in having to make trips to the chiropractor to have my back fixed. With several sets of stairs to clean as well as pathways around the store and adjoined apartment buildings, I had a lot of snow to clean up from each storm.

During the aftermath of one of the big storms, a delivery truck became stuck in the parking lot. The loading dock is located on a downhill slope, it's not steep, but its just enough to cause vehicles to lose traction and struggle to break free. Every year like clockwork at least one truck gets stuck. Being the nice person that I am, I always go out and help dig the driver out and send him on his way. This time I had only spent a few minutes digging and chopping at the ice and snow under the tires to help the truck get traction when I stopped and stepped back to let the driver give it a go. I suddenly became light headed and dizzy. My hearing faded, my vision started to close in and black out, and I became weak in the knees. I instantly drove the shovel into the ground and propped myself up to keep from falling down.

After a minute my vision started to return, my hearing came back, and my head finally stopped spinning. I had no idea what was wrong with me. My first thought was, "How could I have gotten so out of shape in just a few months?" Up until then I had felt fine. Then out of no where I felt like I was going to pass out from just a few minutes of mild labor. I started to wonder if I had a blood pressure problem, but could it come on so suddenly like that? If I did have a blood pressure problem, wouldn't I be having issues all the time? Just as suddenly as it happened, it went away and I felt fine. So, I put it out of my mind.

About three months passed and I had not had another dizzy spell. However, I was a little more tired than usual, and I had developed frequent constipation. At the time I had no idea that this bout of constipation was my first real sign that something very serious and life threatening was wrong with me. Since I have suffered from IBS (Irritable Bowel Syndrome) my whole life, I assumed it was just one of the symptoms of the condition I have learned to live with. When my IBS strikes it causes me to feel very ill, have an upset stomach, mild constipation, or run for the nearest bathroom before my bowels force themselves empty.

This time the constipation I was experiencing didn't seem to go away like it normally did. Frustrated and lost, I finally went to see the doctor and seek advice. I described my symptoms to my doctor and he suggested that I should eat more fiber and change my diet. Willing to try anything, I took his advice. Right after I left the doctor's office, I went straight to the nearest store to stock up on fiber supplements. After a few days I started to return to normal and the pain in my abdomen from the constipation began to decrease.

I thought to myself that for once in my life something was easy and simple. Finally something worked for me! Unfortunately, I could not have been more wrong. My relief was short lived. Within a week I started to get constipated again. I figured since the fiber supplements had worked before, maybe I just needed to increase my dose. However, doing so had the complete opposite effect I had hoped for and the constipation got even worse.

My bowels completely locked up and the pain in my abdomen had returned. I tried adjusting my diet and my fiber intake, but nothing worked. The only thing I could do was take pain relievers just so I could function. At first it worked miracles for me; I would take a few pills and be good for the day, then take a few at night so I could sleep. Over time though the pain grew more and more and I was forced to constantly increase my dose. It got to be so bad that I was literally taking two extra strength pills every three hours day and night around the clock.

I began to feel weak and tired and constantly out of breath no matter how much I rested. My job requires a lot of heavy lifting and other physical labor - everything from carrying around one hundred pound bags of cement, to moving slabs of stone around. I had gotten to the point where just thinking about doing anything physical made me want to collapse. Doing the simplest tasks by now almost seemed impossible.

As time went on, it just continued to get worse. I was starting to get so weak that I could barely make it up the stairs to my own home. By the time I reached the top of a mere single flight of stairs, I was out of breath, light headed, and just dropped into the couch trying desperately to get air into my lungs. I lost my appetite and started dropping unhealthy amounts of weight. The pain had now become unbearable. I was getting almost no sleep and neither was my poor wife. Every night while we tried to sleep I spent most of the time rolling around moaning in pain. The moment I laid down, no matter what position I tried, the pain was excruciating. So each night I would walk laps around the apartment until I was too tired to stand. Some nights I would manage a few hours of sleep. Most nights were spent trying my best to stay quiet so my wife Kellee could rest.

The situation had now become very scary for both my wife and I. I was starting to worry that I might be so sick that I would die. From what, I had no idea, but it was a fear that ran through my mind constantly. My health had become so bad and I was so weak that I could no longer work. I barely had enough energy to get out of bed in the morning and go to the couch in the living room. I spent days lying on the couch drifting in and out of consciousness hoping that whatever this was would soon pass and my life could return to normal.

I finally couldn't take it anymore and consulted my doctor again. After learning of my condition and hearing how bad my pain was, he referred me to a specialist. I set up an appointment with a gastroenterologist to find out exactly what was going on inside my abdomen and to know once and for all what was happening to me. During my visit she proceeded to ask me a series of questions to help pinpoint my problem. After some questions and hearing of what I had been going through, the doctor said it sounded like I either had cancer or Crohn's Disease and some additional tests and scans would be needed to confirm one or the other.

Off and on through this whole ordeal everyone kept telling me I looked pale, some days almost white as a ghost. I attributed it to my just being sick, but the doctor told me that from just looking at me she could tell I was anemic. She then went on to explain that anemia or unexplained blood loss is sometimes a symptom of Crohn's Disease. Though I was in a horrible situation, it gave us something to hope for at the moment. Given the outcome and survival rates of both diseases, I would have gladly chosen Crohn's Disease over cancer any day. As the office visit came to an end, we scheduled an appointment to have my blood tested. It was very imperative that my levels were checked not only to see how much blood I had lost, but to see if there were any signs of other illnesses present.

Normally results for blood tests can take a few days to a week or more depending on what is needed. However, when the lab started testing my blood it was red flagged because the results were so serious. The day after they took my blood I received a phone call from the doctor telling me that I had to make an appointment right away for a blood transfusion. The results of my test showed that my red blood cell count was so low that it was a miracle I was even able to walk around and function. Usually when the counts are this low, people are not able to leave their bed and are barely even conscious. I had managed to stun the doctors at the hospital that I was able to be as functional as I was.

A couple of days later I was in the hospital for the first of several blood transfusions. It was decided from looking at my levels, that I would need a total of four transfusions to get me up to a safe, normal red blood cell count again. The first appointment was to give me two transfusions then wait a few days and check my levels again to see if in fact another two would be fully necessary.

I have never received blood before or given any so this was all new to me. I had been given opportunities in the past to give blood but never volunteered to do so. It wasn't that I was afraid to. It was just one of those things that never really held any importance to me. I see now how mistaken I was, and It's funny how life changing moments like what I was about to go through really make you rethink things like this. The fact that other people were generous enough to donate their blood meant that I would live. It's a touching sentiment to the kindness of humanity (what little still exists in this world) of which I can never tell the people who saved my life, thank you. I can never tell them just how much it means to me, and to my wife, that because of them and their generous gift, I would go on living.

The Crappiest Year Ever

Chapter 4

Receiving Life

Receiving my transfusion was in itself quite an experience. I'm not afraid of needles. I have several tattoos and always get shots when I need them. I just hate being stuck by medical needles of any sort. I've hated it since I was a child, which I'm sure anyone can relate to. You're in a cold room with a strange person poking and prodding you all over, then suddenly they want to stick something sharp into your arm. It's not the fondest of memories. Now not only would I be stuck with a needle, but I would have a tube stuck in my arm for an entire day. I was not a happy camper, but I knew it was necessary, so I grudgingly put up with it.

I seem to have a natural charm with most people and it was once again proven by the fact that all the nurses took an instant liking to me. I look rough on the outside - piercing eyes topped with dark, heavy eyebrows, tattoos...I look like trouble. Add that to the fact that I'm quiet and usually have a stern look on my face, it makes a lot of people want to steer clear of me. Once they actually talk to me, their opinion quickly changes. All of the nurses took turns coming in to check on me and make sure I was okay. Each one spent some time to talking with my wife and I trying to get to know us better. They showed honest concern about my condition which surprised me since my past experiences with most nurses has been unpleasant. Most of them seem to be very bitter, uncaring people which makes you wonder why on earth did they even take on this profession.

In between all the visits, Kellee and I spent the next few hours going back and forth between watching TV and watching the blood drain from the little bag into my body. It wasn't the most exciting day we had ever spent together, but then we weren't expecting any excitement at all, especially what happened next.

After the first transfusion they flushed my I.V. line with saline solution while they waited for the next bag of blood to be retrieved from storage. Before I had started the first bag, the nurses went over precautions and possible allergic reactions and signs to look for. I had no idea how important that would become to me. Like I mentioned earlier, nothing is ever easy or simple for me. If something can go wrong, it usually does.

The next transfusion was set up and the blood began to make its way towards my body. I watched the clear saline solution in the line gradually turn red as the blood pushed its way towards my veins. This time though something was different. Just a few seconds after the blood reached my veins and made its way into my blood stream, something went wrong.

A warm rush suddenly went through my body, my heart started to speed up, I started to feel flush in the face and become a little light headed. I ignored it for a moment to see if it might pass, but it didn't.

I turned to my wife with a stunned, scared look on my face and said "something is wrong, get the nurse!" She looked at me in shock then jumped out of the chair to seek help. By now I was scared something really bad was about to happen so my breathing was even faster and a cold sweat began to break out all over my body. Within seconds one of the nurses came running in and took one look at me and what I was going through and closed off the line. She quickly restarted the saline flush and pushed Benadryl into my system to try to counteract the reaction. Since the Benadryl was going straight to my vein, it actually burned a little as it worked its way through my body. The effects hit me instantly. My pulse slowed down, my breathing began to calm and my body started to relax. After a phone call to my doctor they decided to call it quits for the day and leave me with the one transfusion to give my body a chance to recoup.

Before the transfusion, the low blood counts caused my body to constantly struggle to supply itself with the oxygen and other nutrients it needed in order to function. This was the cause of my weakness and the reason why I was constantly out of breath. Since blood carries oxygen through my system and I had such little blood, I was in a sense suffocating. Any time I had to do anything that required even the slightest bit of effort, there simply wasn't enough blood to supply oxygen where it was needed. This caused me to get weak, light headed, dizzy and in some cases almost black out because my brain was being starved of oxygen.

The most amazing thing was that after having received even just the one transfusion, I felt great, aside from the pain in my abdomen. I didn't feel tired, I had energy again, and even though I was still dangerously low on blood, I felt like a million bucks. When I got home I climbed the stairs to my apartment and made it to the top with out any problem at all. For the first time in a long time my spirits were lifted and even though it was to be short lived, it was exactly what I had needed.

Chapter 5

Discovering The Truth

A few days after the first transfusion, it was time for my colonoscopy. Prior to going in, I was given a prep kit with instructions to get me ready for the procedure. In the prep kit I was given some rather nasty liquid to drink which was to help "cleanse the colon" and clean out all matter that might be present in my digestive system. Since I had to clean out my bowels I was not allowed to eat the day before the procedure, I was only allowed to drink clear liquids. If I knew then what I know now of what was about to become of all this, I would have made my last meal something grander than what it was. Reluctantly I drank the laxative and prepared myself as much as I could for the colonoscopy.

The next morning rolled around and we set off to the hospital to have a look inside me and hopefully once and for all figure out what was wrong with me. Once there I was greeted by the same nurses from my last visit, they showed me to my room and told me to put on one of those wonderfully, annoying hospital gowns and climb into the bed. Shortly after, the anesthesiologist came into my room and introduced himself, he started to go over the procedure with me and explain the types of drugs he was about to put into me which would put me to sleep.

By now I was starting to get nervous. I had never been in the hospital ever in my life to have anything done with the exception of the blood transfusion I had done the week before. He assured me I would be taken care of, and I would feel no pain at all from start to finish and that it would only take 15-20 minutes from the time I went to sleep.

I was then rolled down the long cold hallways of the hospital to the operating room. I was greeted by the doctor who was going to do the procedure as well as the other staff. They all did their best to comfort me and explain the process and reassure me that everything will be okay. They then asked me to slide over from my bed to the examining table and lay on my side. An I.V. was put into my arm and my bare butt was exposed.

Moments later the camera was activated and I saw the first ever glimpse of my butt on a TV screen, hopefully to be the last. I was told to relax and breathe normally and to expect my eyelids to start to get heavy once the first push of the anesthesia was administered. I looked over at the anesthesiologist and saw a giant syringe filled with a milky looking substance, he slowly pushed in half of the liquid and sure enough my eyelids started to become heavy. Seeing that I was okay he gave the final push, I saw his hand move and the liquid start to go though the tube. Then everything went black, total and complete blackness. Interestingly though, my other senses didn't completely go away. I could still hear the beep from the heart rate machine. I couldn't really think, I had no dreams, no real thoughts of any kind. All I knew was that I was aware of the constant beep from my heart on the machine.

The next thing I knew I was waking up in a different room I had never seen before. It turned out to be part of the recovery area where they monitor people right after they undergo any kind of surgery or procedure. I had a new nurse sitting next to my bed watching my monitors and making sure I didn't suddenly crash and die.

When I woke I didn't feel woozy or tired or like I had been drugged. It felt like I had just blinked for a really long time. My eyes danced around the room looking at everything, trying to absorb what had just happened and where I was. The nurse noticed I was awake and asked me if everything was okay. I told her I was fine but then asked if it was normal to hear things while being under. With a puzzled look on her face she asked what I meant. I explained how I remembered hearing the heart rate machine the whole time I was under. A small smile appeared on her face and she said it was normal and that some patients do experience that. Feeling more confident that it was nothing to worry about, I relaxed and waited to be taken back to my room.

After about 20 minutes had passed they were confident I was okay, and I was returned back to my original room in the hospital where Kellee was waiting for me. Once there I was told I could get dressed again when I was ready and that the doctor would be in soon to discuss my results. I waited in my bed for awhile to make sure that all of the drugs had completely worn off. The last thing I wanted was to stand up from the bed and take a nose dive into the wall or some sharp piece of furniture.

A few minutes had passed while I lie in bed talking to Kellee when the doctor came in. You can almost always tell whether it's good or bad news by simply looking at doctors' faces, and I could tell it wasn't good. With a glum look on his face and all around depressing demeanor, he sat in a chair at the foot of my bed. With my wife by my side he began to explain what he had found and how my life would be changed forever.

The doctor explained that while doing my procedure he had found a rather large blockage in my large intestine which looked to be a tumor. This was of course the cause of all my pain and discomfort. Due to the size of it, the growth had almost completely closed off my intestines which was causing me to be constipated. And as it turned out, the growth was also the cause for my blood loss. While examining me, they took a biopsy of the tissue for further study to see what exactly it was.

Regardless of what the growth was, due to the severity of the situation and the fact that my colon was so close to being closed off completely, I had to have surgery to have it removed. He told us that the opening in my colon was so small he couldn't even get the small camera through to explore further. If we had waited any longer it would have completely closed off and I could have died if I didn't bleed to death first.

An utter feeling of despair came over me, the thought of having to undergo actual surgery has always been something I feared and never wanted to face. I was given two options regarding the surgery, the first being that since I had already done the colonoscopy prep and that my bowels were empty, I could continue to fast for a few more days then go into surgery, or I could go back to eating and schedule the surgery for another time. The second choice would mean that I would have to do the prep all over again and drink more of that nasty bowel emptying liquid. Facing up to my fears, and reluctantly saying goodbye to all food I agreed to schedule the surgery for as soon as possible. It was apparent to me that my life was in serious danger, and I had to face my fear and do what was needed to save my life.

I suppose my reason for being afraid of surgery came from the fact that I learned one day that some people who undergo surgery, despite being given anesthesia to sleep, end up being aware and feeling every moment of the surgery. They feel every cut, every tug, every last painful experience of it, yet can do nothing to stop it. I had the unnerving feeling that with my horrible luck in life I would end up being one of those people. Overcoming my fear, I pushed the thought out of my head as much as I could and made the appointment for two days later.

After the doctor left my room, I proceeded to get dressed and get ready to go home and let all the news soak in, but the people at the hospital had other plans for me. Without my knowledge, they had scheduled the rest of my blood transfusions for the same day because they had to get as much blood in me as possible to prepare for the surgery. My wife Kellee and I were a little upset by this news since it was unknown to us and we hadn't been prepared at all for it, but understanding the issues at hand we had no choice. Once again I was placed in the chair and had yet another needle shoved into my arm - something that I was going to have to get very used to whether I liked it or not.

So there I was once again, propped up in the chair having a needle stuck into my arm. Just like last time my wife and I sat and watched the blood drain into me over the next couple of hours. Once the first bag was done, they again did the saline flush to prepare me for the next bag which was on its way. Oddly enough, just like last time, as soon as the second transfusion reached my arm I started to have another negative reaction to it. I quickly told my wife who again went running for the nurse. A few seconds later she came running in and once again stopped the line and flushed it with saline.

Confused about my odd pattern of rejection they sent the blood off for testing to make sure it was the right blood type for me. It turned out the blood was fine and they could not explain my reaction. After some discussion they decided to try it again, this time however they would push Benadryl into my system to try and counteract any allergic reactions I might have. Once again, my veins were on fire as the Benadryl worked its way through my system. My body relaxed, my breathing eased and we gave it another try. This time the transfusion finally went okay with out any further issues.

After a few hours the transfusion was done and it was time to go home. The nurses disconnected the I.V and we then gathered our stuff to head home. The next day when the results came back we learned that I did in fact have colon cancer. Now not only would I need surgery to remove the tumor, I would also need chemotherapy as well. It was disconcerting news which would take several days to really sink in, and when it finally did, I began to seriously fear for my life.

Chapter 6

Losing Hope

During this whole ordeal my condition really put a strain on my relationship with my wife. We both had fears of what might happen. Kellee's biggest fear of course was that I might die. She is the type of person that faces all issues the same way no matter how small and trivial they might be. Every problem is suddenly the end of the world. Being the rock that I am (which is how my mother-in-law Carol refers to me), I do my best to keep her calm and help relieve her of stress as much as possible and assure her that everything will be okay.

Granted this wasn't a small matter, but I did everything I could to keep her as positive as I have been through this whole ordeal. It's not an easy task by any means to keep myself positive or my wife for that matter, but it's what keeps me going. I do everything I can in my power to make her happy because it's what's most important to me. I want her to be happy. I want her to smile and not have her worry about me.

Not to say that I myself didn't have fears that I might soon face the end of my short, yet enjoyed life. Despite the fact that I had been dealt a pretty crappy hand in life I found a way to make it past the depression and eventually find a way to move on in life and accept fate and find happiness where and when I can.

Kellee has always been lost in the fact that I hardly ever seem to stress over certain situations. She can't seem to understand how I never let problems bother me. Though it might seem that way, it is untrue. I do in fact stress over and worry about various problems. The difference is that I don't let it last very long. Yes, bad stuff happens to me, but I have so many other things in my life to be grateful for.

My basic outlook on life is that despite what bad things may happen, I focus on the good and not the bad. Even if it means finding joy in something small and dumb that most people couldn't care less about. A perfect example of this is my love for tacos (soft shell, tex mex style) and how excited I get when I plan to make it for a dinner on a specific evening. I not only love the taste of it, but it's tied together with memories of my childhood. For many birthdays growing up, we always had the choice of whatever we wanted for dinner on our "special day". My brother Curt and I always seemed to choose tacos. So when I decide to make it, all week long I look forward to it. It's my little coveted treasure that brings happiness to my life. So I find happiness where I can from whatever I can. What good will stressing over something do for me? None at all, it won't make the situation any better, it won't fix it and make it go away. So why let it ruin and run my life?

Even though I can find some kind of good in my life no matter how bad something might be that doesn't mean the stress of any given situation doesn't get to me on occasion. In seeing how bad my health had gotten before we knew of the cancer, the idea that I might in fact die soon had become a real thought in my head. I spent many days thinking about my life and whether or not I was happy with the outcome. If I did die, would I die happy? Would I feel that I had lived a good enough life up until now? Could I go with out any regrets?

I spent many nights laying restless in bed thinking about my life and my possible death. I was able to ease my fears with thoughts of being surrounded by my loved ones in the end and being with those who truly cared about me and saying one last goodbye to them. I never spoke of any of this to anyone. I didn't want them to worry any more than they already did. I did what I always do, I found something to be happy about and in turn this helped to ease others' fears. After all if I seemed happy and content, it made everyone else less likely to worry.

Eventually, I came to the conclusion that no matter what one does in life there will always be some regrets. I found myself wishing I had gone here, done this, or done that. Yes, there were things I wished I had done, but in the end I was satisfied with what I had achieved and accomplished in my life thus far. I had come to terms with the fact that I might die and that if I did, I could be at peace. I married an amazing woman who means the world to me, I have a good home, a loving family, I had traveled a little, and seen some amazing sights. Sure there was still a mile long bucket list, but in the end, I could live with out them and just leave them as dreams.

There were a few times where it just became a little too over whelming that I just couldn't hold the fears in anymore. The first time was before I had my initial appointment with the gastroenterologist when I called my mother to let her know that something was wrong and to prepare both her and my dad for what might be a short lived future for me. Of course I made no mention of the fact that I might die, but I couldn't hold back all of my emotions as I informed my mother that I may be facing a battle with cancer. I could tell she was as worried as I was while talking with her on the phone. As I explained my situation I could hear her getting choked up as she spoke, which as a result I started to get choked up too. I did the best I could to ease her fears and let her know that her baby boy would be okay.

I knew my mom understood the situation better than anyone else. She had spent the last 10 years of her life battling cancer. First, she was stuck with cancer of the uterus, then twice with colon cancer. All three times she won, but I am sure that just like me, she had to face the fears that she might not survive through it. The fact that she herself had gone through it, made her one of my biggest inspirations, my shining light to look towards when things got darkest. If she could beat it, so could I.

Chapter 7

Going Under The Knife

The days between my colonoscopy and my surgery seemed like an eternity. It was made even worse by the fact that I could not eat solid food. I was restricted to a liquids only diet, which for a day is okay, but more than that is awful. Breakfast became a bottle of Gatorade, lunch and dinner consisted of either beef or chicken broth, and in between I tried to mix things up with either popsicles or Jello.

Each meal had become pure torture. I would sit and choke down my broth as I watched my wife eat real food. I felt like a starving orphan boy watching some witch eat a grand buffet in front of me just to torture me while I starved. My wife of course felt bad and never intentionally tried to make me suffer, but when you're in that position, even the smallest morsel, looks like a meal fit for a king. Never in my life had I experienced such longing for food.

The day before my surgery my fears really began to settle in and grew more as the day went on. I did what I could to try and keep my stress levels down, but there was only so much I or anyone could do to keep me from worrying myself sick. That evening I received quite a surprise which for a short while took my mind off of my upcoming surgery. One by one I received phone calls from my parents and all of my brothers. Each one took the time to call me and reassure me that everything would be okay and that they would be waiting by the phone after my surgery to make sure everything went as planned. They all did their best to cheer me up and help put my mind at ease. They will probably never know how much it meant to me that they called. My brothers and I were never really that close. So, it was a huge surprise to see that they cared enough to call and make sure their little brother was going to be okay.

That night I did my best to get as much rest as possible before my surgery, I went to bed starving and my stomach growling. I was forbidden from eating or drinking anything past mid afternoon the day before the surgery. I was starting to feel like if the tumor didn't kill me I would soon starve to death.

That night my mind raced like crazy and real fear had started to set in. What if I am one of those people who feels everything during surgery? What if something goes wrong, what if I die? Needless to say I slept very little that night.

The next morning when we awoke, my wife and we did our best to keep each other's mood up as we got ready to head out. It was decided that my mother-in-law was going to drive us to the hospital and stay with Kellee to keep her company while I was operated on.

I didn't say much on the drive to the hospital. Kellee sat in the back seat with me and held my hand. Although this was somewhat comforting, I could not shake my fear of the unknown. The whole ride down I just stared out the car window dreading reaching my destination. My wife and her mother made small talk during the drive and tried to include me, but I found very few words to say no matter what the subject.

Upon arriving at the hospital, the reality of the situation started to set in, within a few hours I was going to be laying on a table, my stomach sliced open, and my intestines yanked out and cut to pieces. I tried to keep myself calm, but given the situation it became harder as time passed.

Before I knew it, I was in my hospital gown lying in my bed waiting for my time to come. Eventually the anesthesiologist, the same one I had dealt with before, entered my room to talk with me once again about the procedure to come, and what kind of anesthesia process I wanted to do. My two options were an epidural where they would place an I.V. line into my lower spine or a normal intravenous line which would go in my arm. He explained to me that the epidural is the better of the two mainly because it would be releasing the anti-pain medicine directly to the area where I would be hurting the most, where as the I.V. line would just be a drip bag connected to my arm and that the pain medicine would have to travel through my whole body before it finally made it's way to my abdomen.

At first I was very against the epidural because I was under the impression that I would have a needle stuck in my back for a week and I was afraid that I might move it and make things worse or end up paralyzing myself. As I talked to the anesthesiologist he told me that the needle would only be in my body initially just to get the I.V. line into my spine and then it would be retracted. Prior to doing this (since it would be very painful) they would inject me with a general anesthesia to make the process less painful. After thinking it over, I agreed and signed a waiver for the epidural.

Again I waited for what seemed like forever. I lay in my bed talking with my wife and mother in law doing my best to keep my mind off of what was to come. Eventually the nurse came to take me to the operating room. I said goodbye to my wife and my mother-in-law and parted ways. I was once again pushed down the long cold hallways of the hospital while I lie in my bed. The man who was pushing my bed recognized me from last time and did his best to make small talk with me to put my mind at ease.

We made our way to the room I had woken up in before when I had my colonoscopy done. I was met there by the anesthesiologist and it was now time to insert the epidural line. They had me sit up in bed and lean forward, they then explained that I would feel a lot of pressure and maybe a little pain in my lower back, but it would be quick. I can't even imagine how much it would have hurt if they hadn't given me something to numb the area prior to inserting the epidural into my spine. I felt the pressure they had mentioned along with a sudden surge of pain. I winced and groaned with distain, but thankfully it was over fairly quickly. They taped the lines to my back and had me lay down once again to regain my composure. Moments later I was then wheeled out and into the operating room.

I was more scared now than I have ever been in my life. Was this real? Is this some sort of nightmare? Will I suddenly wake up and everything will be fine? As much as I had wished it was all a dream, it was real. I was about to have someone take a knife to my stomach and cut me open.

Inside the operating room I was greeted by the surgeon and the nurses as they positioned me next to the operating table. Unlike what you might see in the movies, I was not picked up and placed on the table, rather they had me sit up and slide over onto the table. I remember finding it odd that you always see them lift the patients on and off the table but for me I had to make my own way to my destination.

My eyes looked stressfully around the room trying to find something to focus on to calm my nerves. Unfortunately, they found nothing. The doctors and the nurses worked around me prepping me for the surgery, shoving more lines into me, and explaining that they would have to put a tube down my throat, as well as one up my urethra. The tube that was going down my throat was going to deflate my stomach and help keep me from getting nauseous after the surgery. It would also help stifle hunger pains since I would not be eating for several days after my surgery. The one that went into my urethra was to drain urine out of me as needed. Luckily those two were not to be done until I was unconscious.

A few minutes later and the anesthesiologist was again my by side. He took a moment to show me and explain the different drugs that he would be using. I honestly had no real idea of what he was saying. I was so nervous and upset that I just nodded my head as he talked to show that I understood him even though I didn't. When he finished, another doctor appeared by my side and told me he was going to put an oxygen mask over my mouth and nose and to just breathe normally. After a few short breaths everything went black.

Next thing I knew I woke up and I was still on the operating table, after a moment of confusion had passed I realized I had not woken up in the ICU like before but instead I was still on the table. I looked around in absolute fear to try and figure out what was going on when my eyes caught site of the surgeon. I noticed everyone else had disappeared but he was still there. I watched him for a moment trying to figure out what was happening, after a moment I realized he was cleaning up. A brief second of calm entered my head as I realized that the anesthesia had worn off a little early and the operation was over. I was so relived that I had not woken up during the procedure.

Still in a daze, I looked all around the room trying to figure out what was going on, when suddenly, feeling returned to my body. I was aware of being freezing cold and shivering. Then suddenly I noticed the immense pain in my abdomen. As if the pain itself wasn't bad enough, the fact that I was shivering and shaking made it even worse. My whole body shook, my muscles every where were tense and it all made the pain that much worse.

As I laid there shaking, the nurses had returned and helped the doctor lift me off the table and back onto my bed. I was so glad they had lifted me. I was afraid they were going to ask me to crawl over myself, but to my relief they didn't. Though it hurt immensely, I was still grateful that I did not have to try and move over by myself.

I was taken from the operating room back into recovery where once again a nurse waited by my side to watch all my vitals and make sure I was okay. They had put a blanket over me to help me warm up, but I was still freezing. I had spent the last several hours in an ice cold room with nothing to keep me warm. I was frozen from head to toe. I could no longer take the pain that the shivering was causing me, so I mustered up every bit of strength I had to ask for help. All I could do was barely mumble the word cold. The nurse hearing me say something turned to my attention and asked me what I had said. Shaking uncontrollably I once again muttered the word cold. She got up quickly and came back with a preheated blanket which she gingerly draped over my body. I could feel the warmth instantly, it felt so unbelievably good and finally my shivering was starting to subside.

I spent about a half hour in the recovery area before they finally wheeled me to my new room in the ICU. Shortly thereafter, they let my wife and mother-in-law come in to visit me. I was greeted with smiles from both of them, their minds were put to rest at seeing me and knowing that everything went as planned. In my weakened state, I couldn't talk much but then I wasn't sure I had much to say. I was just glad I had made it through and that I wasn't one of those poor souls who experience every moment of their surgery despite being knocked out.

My wife and her mother didn't stay long. They spent just enough time to make sure I was okay before bidding me farewell to get my rest. Kellee would later tell me that just before the surgeon came out to tell her that everything was okay, she looked out the window in the lobby and just as her eyes focused on the world outside, the clouds gave way and the sun appeared. It had been dark and gloomy all day and now just before the surgeon came to see them the sun had broken through the clouds brighter and more beautiful than ever. She says that when she saw the sun shining she knew everything was okay and that I would be fine. Then moments later the doctor appeared and had confirmed her premonition.

To her it was the universe, maybe God himself, telling her that she did not have to worry anymore. All her fears could be put to rest and her husband would be okay. It could have all been a coincidence or it could have been divine intervention. No one will ever know, but it's a comforting thought to think that someone is out there looking over us.

Chapter 8

I'm In Hell

I drifted in and out of sleep during my first night in the hospital. The pain from the tumor that was once inside me was gone, but now I was in pain from my surgery. I was given a button to push that released pain medicine into my epidural for when the pain became too much to bare. At first I was reluctant to push it too often, I didn't want the nurses to judge me and think I was some sort of drug addict. So for my first night and most of the next day I suffered.

One might ask why I would let myself suffer like that. Well it didn't help that my first nurse was a very unpleasant woman with an attitude, and while handing me the button she told me it was for the pain but not to use it too often. She said it with a condescending tone in her voice making it seem like she thought I would be pushing it all the time to try and get high. I don't like people thinking things like that about me. I have spent most of my life having people be afraid of me because of how I look. I have been told time and time again, even by complete strangers that I look mean. In truth, I am the complete opposite. I am the nicest person one could ever meet. I hate being prejudged, so just like in other situations I suffered to prove people wrong.

I spent much of my first day in the hospital drifting in and out of sleep and catching up on day time television. There wasn't much else I could do, I could barely move and I had no one to talk to until my wife came to visit me. Every moment that she had free, she spent by my side while I recovered. Even though I mostly slept while she was there, it didn't matter. She just wanted to be close to me, and it was a soothing thought for me knowing she was there.

As the evening drew near Kellee felt it was getting late and she decided to head home. We said our goodbyes and she left with a smile on her face. I settled into bed watching TV trying to get as comfortable as possible so that I might finally sleep the night through. If I had known what was in store for me I would not have bothered. I would have instead pushed the button for the pain meds ahead of time to make what was about to happen easier on me.

The mean nurse was back; she came into my room and told me that it was time for her to clean me. At first it seemed like an okay idea, I hadn't bathed in about a day, so I was happy to oblige. At first things seemed to be okay, she pulled my blanket back here and there to clean me with out fully exposing me to the world.

It was a refreshing change, I was being bathed and the cool temperature of the wipes was very soothing. All of that was short lived though, a male nurse entered and they told that they had to flip me onto my side to clean the back of me and change my gown. The first thought that entered my mind was dear god this is going to hurt, and then suddenly it turned to fear. What if my stitches tear, what if my wound rips open and my intestines start to seep out.

Before I could get a grip on the situation they were both on opposite sides of the bed. They told me to grab the bar on the side of the bed and pull myself toward it while one would push me up and the other would pull. The pain was immense, I squeezed my eyes shut and groaned in pain. I had never felt anything like this before, and it was just the beginning.

Suddenly I felt like I was in the movie Fight Club, I became **Travis/Rupert**. I kept my eyes closed and tried to find my happy place. I tried to shut out the pain and put my mind else where. I thought of my wife. I thought of our favorite vacation place and our honeymoon in Hawaii. After what seemed like an eternity it was finally finished, and I was laid back down dressed in a new hospital gown. Breathing heavily, I laid there waiting for my body to recover from what it had just endured, but it was only the beginning. When they finished dressing me they told me that they once again had to prop me on my side, only this time I would be staying like that.

Clenching my eyes shut once again I gritted my teeth and prepared for the pain. I grabbed onto the bar on the side of my bed and pulled while they pushed and pulled me onto my left side and shoved pillows behind me to help hold me up. I leaned back into the pillows groaning from the pain, if I had only known I would have pushed the button sooner. They put my blankets back over me and handed me my button, I pushed it the moment it was in my hand, but it was too late, the pain was so great that the medicine was almost too weak to counteract it. A few minutes after pushing the button it gave me just barely enough relief to make the pain bearable. I closed my eyes thinking it was over and passed out.

Again I was proven wrong. A few hours later, I was woken up and informed they were going to change my position again. This time, in anticipation I said in my head screw this, I don't care what they think, this is going to hurt, so I pushed the button once more. The medicine pumped into my back as they began to prep me. I reluctantly grabbed onto the bar on the side of my bed while they pulled me over to remove the pillows. I tried desperately to slowly lower myself onto my back, but I was too weak to hold myself and I fell onto my back in the bed. I groaned and fought to catch my breath, the pain was worse after having let myself fall back into the bed.

I lay there praying this was it and that I could try to relax but more was still to come. The mean nurse told me to get ready to flip onto my right side. I began to think to myself, "How can they do this to me? Why won't they just leave me alone? Can't they see that I am in pain? Just a little over 24 hours ago my stomach was sliced open! Give me a break!

Between my groans I begged them to leave me alone. I told them how much it hurts and to just go away. She told me it was for my own good, my back was red and I could develop bed sores if they don't move me. At this point I didn't care. I was in pain and I just wanted to be left alone, but they wouldn't leave until they turned me. I took a minute to ready myself - I grabbed onto the bar, took a small breath, and pulled myself up with their help. They shoved the pillows behind me and laid me back onto them.

Laying on my right hurt so much more than my left - I had no idea why at the time, but in the future I would find out that the large intestines are actually attached to the inner wall of the abdomen, where as the small intestines are not. The small intestines are left free to move around and fill in any gaps. Having had my large intestines removed from the right side of my body, my small intestines were free to move in and fill the gap there. Laying on my right also tugged slightly on the left side of my large intestines since it was still attached to my abdomen wall as well as the spot where they reconnected my small and large intestines back together.

Needless to say, I didn't get any sleep while propped up on my right side, the pain was too much and nothing helped. I laid there for a few hours just staring blankly, doing my best to get lost in my own thoughts. I was somewhat reminded of a music video which has references to an old war movie about a battle-wounded soldier who was trapped in his own body with no way to communicate. Like him, my mind drifted all over trying to find anything that could take my thoughts away from the reality I was currently in.

I laid there for what seemed like forever when I heard my door open again. "Dear God no," I thought to myself, "Not again, no more, please no more." They had returned once again to move me. Why couldn't they just leave me be? The mean nurse told me it was time to put me on to my back again. "Thank God," I thought, "Finally a position that won't hurt me." Unfortunately, in order to get there I had to put myself through hell again. I pushed the button once more and gave the medicine a few minutes to work its way through my body. Feeling like I could handle it, I grabbed onto the bed and pulled myself up. It hurt a lot, but I was starting to get used to the pain. They removed the pillows from me and helped me slowly roll on to my back. Finally I was in a position that didn't cause me excessive pain. After they left, I closed my eyes and soon went to sleep.

Chapter 9

Past Revisited

The next few days in the ICU were a bit of a blur. Between being on medication and weak from the surgery, I was constantly drifting in and out of consciousness. I was always aware when my wife or others came to visit though. I would save all my energy for my visitors so I could be awake when they came and finally have someone to talk to. I greeted everyone with a smile as best I could. I was thankful to be alive, and grateful to have people that cared about me enough to visit me and make sure I was okay.

On one of the days in the ICU I had enough strength to finally make phone calls to my relatives and spend some time updating them on my condition. The first call was of course to my parents, I talked with both my mom and dad for some time, letting them know I was okay and how much I couldn't wait to be able to eat real food again and finally get out of the hospital.

That call however left me a little upset. My wife swears that I was angry with my mother. I will agree that I wasn't happy with the outcome of the call, but I certainly wasn't angry at her. I was more disappointed than anything. I had called my mom looking for a good sympathetic conversation. However, most of the conversation was one sided and almost all of her responses were just simple one word replies. I was in the hospital, in pain, suffering, and all I wanted to be consoled by my mother just like a child when they scrape their knee.

It wasn't anything new to have similar conversations with my mother on the phone like this, but I suppose I wished this time it would have been different. Later in time while talking with my father I found out it wasn't just with me that this happened. He explained to me that my mom had become like that with everyone on the phone. Why? Honestly, no one knew. My only guess is that the time my mother had spent dealing with her own health issues had somewhat changed her personality, possibly even left her a little more bitter towards life. Perhaps dealing with all of it, had taken away a little of her spark and made her want to close her self out from the world.

My mother and I have shared similar lives in the sense that we both had bad luck in life. However, her hardships growing up were much worse than anything I ever experienced. Her real father was an alcoholic and died when she was young. Her real mother was a horrible woman and wanted nothing to do with her own kids and put them up for adoption.

My mother was adopted when she was young, but the pain didn't stop there. My "grandparents" had adopted her because at the time it was thought they couldn't have kids of their own. My grandfather treated her as if she was his own, and he never left her wanting for love. My grandmother on the other hand always had some sort of bitterness towards her. She was a lot harder on her, punished her more, and I'm sure didn't always show her the love she deserved.

After some time, my grandparents were finally able to have a child of their own. Although they were happy, the situation only made matters worse for my mother. She was always punished for what her "sister" did. Her "sister" was always the good one and she was the bad child, at least in my grandmother's eyes. Despite this, my grandfather did his best to let my mother know that she was always loved. At times, my grandmother would punish her and send her to bed with out dinner and my grandfather would sneak into her room and give her something to eat and console her.

I don't know why, but they pushed her so hard to make her what they wanted her to be and not what she wanted to be. My grandparents are very religious people and pushed my mother hard to be like them to the point that she almost became a nun for them. I am grateful on many levels that this did not happen. First of all, she would have been miserable, and second, I would have never been born.

I remember the time when I first found out about what my mother had been put through. Every year around March, my parents would make the trek up from Virginia to Pennsylvania for a bit of a family reunion. Two of my brothers still lived in Pennsylvania and my other brother moved back to Long Island, NY where we all lived as children, and I had moved to Connecticut. Pennsylvania was easy enough for my other brother and I to get to and since two already lived there it seemed like the right place to meet. So, every year in one form or another we all either met at the same time or took times spending a few days with my parents.

This particular year was one of the few times when we managed to get the whole family together. All four sons, their wives and their kids, all crammed together in one timeshare for a day filled of stories, laughs and food. Things went as they normally did - we exchanged funny stories about doing our best to embarrass each other growing up. We ate home-cooked food made by our mother which was something we rarely had the chance to experience any more, and just all around having a fun time.

I don't really remember how the topic came up, but at one point someone had asked my father about my mother and her parents. My father, being the big talker that he is, launched into the whole story of her growing up and all of the emotional pain and hardships she had to endure. I was shocked to hear about how my mother was treated. In my whole life I never had any idea of what she had gone through. While listening to my father tell the story, I looked over at my mother and saw a blank lost look on her face as she listened to my father speak. I could tell she was stuck in her own memories and fighting away the pain that they brought about.

My heart sank as I watched her. To think of my mother going through all this pain brought about a huge sadness in me. Never had I wished so hard that I could make things right for her. Thankfully, after some time she was able to snap out of it and realize that she was surrounded by her real family - her loving husband, her four sons, and their wives and kids. All of whom loved her unconditionally and would do anything for her at the drop of a hat. Soon enough the smile came back as she looked at all of us and realized she had many things to be happy about.

I'm glad to say that despite the hardships she had dealt with growing up, she never gave in, she pushed on and persevered. I guess in many ways I am just like my mother when it comes to things like that. She gave me her strength and her "never-give-up" attitude. We are fighters to the bitter end.

Chapter 10

First Steps

After a couple days in the ICU, my condition was improving faster than the doctor's expectations. They soon started removing tubes from me and started to push me harder towards recovering. They removed the tube that was going into my stomach and the one that was going up my urethra. This meant I was now allowed to start taking liquids into my body. Food, however, was still days away. As much as I was dying for a solid meal, the fact that I could now drink (though in small doses) was better than nothing, and I was excited to finally taste something other than my own saliva.

I was given as many cups of ice chips as I wanted, this was far from a grand meal but to me it was a gracious moment and I was soon chomping away like a starving man at an all you can eat buffet. It felt so good to feel the cool liquid trickle past my tongue and down my throat. Though I was hydrated from the I.V. the sensation of actually taking in fluids after so many days without, can only be described as heaven. It's amazing how something as simple as chewing on ice chips can mean so much now, when on any given day in the past it would have meant nothing at all.

While I sat with a smile in my bed eating my ice and feeling great, a nurse had entered and told me that the doctor ordered that I try and get out of bed and move to a chair. This was part of the push to speed up my recovery. With their help I was to get up out of bed and walk over to a chair and sit. This was to help get back my strength in my legs so I could walk, and to change my position. I was not at all prepared for what was about to happen. Before they could move me they had to also remove the epidural from my back. This was to be the end of instant pain relief, and to be replaced with an I.V. drip with pain meds and eventually when I could eat to be switched to pills.

I put my cup of ice chips down and used the motors in the bed to help sit me up, I leaned forward and let the doctor remove the epidural, it wasn't the most pleasant feeling in the world, but I was in a sense glad to have it gone.

Now ready for the big move I pulled my blankets aside, being careful not to pull my gown with it and expose myself to everyone in the room. I took a few deep breaths and tried to ready myself to make the big move. Something was wrong though, I couldn't move my legs. Try as I might, they wouldn't respond. I reached down and touched them and felt nothing. My legs were completely numb. I could wiggle my toes fine but I could not lift either leg the slightest.

The nurses asked me what was wrong and I told them I couldn't feel my legs or make them move. To my relief, they told me this happens sometimes and that's why it's important I get out of the bed and move. It turned out that not only had some of the nerves gone to sleep from being in the same position for so long, but the pain medicine had been pooling in my legs and made them go completely numb. I was told I wouldn't be able to walk on my own for a few days, but with their help I had to at least get out of the bed and sit in the chair even if just for a short while.

With one nurse on each side of me, they lifted my legs and slowly turned me until my legs were left dangling over the side. It was now that I was sorry to see my epidural gone, the pain was intense, but I could handle it. With another deep breath, they slid me closer to the edge of the bed until my feet hit the floor. With one nurse still on each side of me, they pulled to get me to my feet. As if I had no legs at all, I instantly dropped down and they both struggled to hold me up. With no feeling in my legs I could not control the muscles at all and it turned me into nothing but dead weight. Pulling up on them I steadied myself as much as I could and wobbled, dipped, and bowed as I moved the two steps to the chair. Once there I collapsed hard into it with both relief and pain. Never in my life have I thought that someday I would have trouble walking like this.

Out of breath from the struggle, I lifted myself up a little with my arms to get myself as comfortable as I could. Once I was settled, the nurses left and my wife was allowed to come back in. They told us they would be back later to get me back in to bed. I sat there for a moment wondering if getting back in to bed was going to be just as hard as it was to get out.

Kellee and I sat and chatted for a bit, she told me about her day and updated me on news about work and people and family. As always it was the highlight of my day, not only did I finally have someone to talk to, but I could spend time with my wife. I had missed her dearly and it was great to spend some time with her and see that beautiful smile that makes my heart flutter.

After about an hour or so the nurses returned to get me back in bed. Just like before, it took both of them to get me standing and hold me up long enough to shuffle me back to the bed. It took every bit of strength I had left to push and pull myself back into the bed. By the time it was done, I was in immense pain again. I was exhausted, in pain, and ready to just pass out. Seeing this, my wife tucked me in and said goodbye for the evening. I watched TV for awhile and ate my ice chips while waiting for the pain to subside enough for me to sleep. Much needed sleep finally came.

Chapter 11

A Room With A View

I was in the ICU for about 3-4 days after my surgery. Once I could be moved in and out of bed, it was time for me to leave and head to another section of the hospital. I was going to my room where I would spend the rest of my stay. It was a bit of a shock when a nurse entered and told me it was time to take me to my room. The first thought that came to my mind was, how am I going to get there? Are they going to wheel me in the bed? Are they going to try and make me walk it? Or maybe a wheelchair? Of course my next thought was here comes more pain.

At that moment, before real thoughts could settle in, the nurse answered my question by bringing in a wheelchair. Knowing now what I had to do, I once again braced myself for another big move. Despite the constant I.V. drip of pain medicine, the pain was always mildly present. Big moves like this were always more than what the pain meds could buffer. So, it took a lot of mental preparation to get myself through. After all, the only thing holding my stomach closed at this point was a line of staples down my abdomen. Any time I made a move it always tugged on the area and brought about extreme pain.

The nurse positioned the wheelchair close to the bed and helped rotate me to the edge. My legs had gained back some of their strength and mobility by now, but I was still very weak and still had a lot of trouble moving without help. Holding tightly onto her arm and bracing myself, I slowly slid myself off the edge of the bed to my feet. My legs shook and jittered around as I shuffled my way to the wheel chair. While holding tightly onto the nurse's arm, I slowly lowered into the wheelchair.

After setting up my I.V. bag for the trip and tucking a blanket around me, we were on our way. This was the first time I had seen anything other than the four walls of my ICU room in days. I was excited; finally I am leaving this spot and hopefully going some where better. A rush of fresh air brushed across my face as we made our way down the hallway. I felt like a dog in a car sticking its head out the window while the car drives along. Although slight, the breeze felt so good. My eyes danced in every direction soaking up my surroundings. To most people it would be just another boring, drab hallway. To me, it was freedom. It was something new. It was an escape.

Heading into an elevator we went up to the next floor. When we exited the elevator, I was greeted by the new nurses at their station as we passed by. We turned a corner into my room and a giant sigh of relief came over me. I saw only one bed and a whole wall of windows. Not only would I have the room to myself and all the privacy I wanted, but I had one heck of a view. My room over looked part of the roof of the hospital, but beyond that was a beautiful field, rolling hills, and a mountain off in the distance. My love of hiking and nature made this the perfect treat.

I was wheeled over to the bed, and with the help of the nurse, I was once again on my feet dragging them across the floor with all my strength to get me into my new bed. I used my arms to pull myself into the bed while the nurse lifted my feet. The nurse then proceeded to get me settled in my new temporary home. I was given my TV remote, my call button, and my cup of ice chips. At that moment I wasn't interested in my
TV or my ice chips. I just laid there and stared out the window at my view. I hadn't seen the outside world in days. I had been cooped up in a windowless room in hell with nothing but pain as my companion. I closed my eyes for a moment and imagined myself walking around in that field, feeling the sun on my skin and the breeze across my face. It didn't matter why I was there or what I was doing, I was free and enjoying every moment of it.

Opening my eyes, I was thrust back into reality. I noticed the nurse was setting up a bunch of toiletries for me, as well as a breathing exercise machine. This little breathing exerciser was to be my new pal for the rest of my stay. I was told to use it through out the day, every day, for a few minutes each time. It was to help build up my abdominal strength, lung strength, and help keep any infections from setting into my lungs.

It was a simple plastic device with a tube sticking out of it. It reminded me a lot of the breathalyzer that cops use when doing sobriety tests on drunk drivers. The main differences were that, obviously, I was not drunk, and that I was supposed to take deep breaths in versus breathing out. It had a gauge in the middle that measured how much force I pulled in with my lungs. My job was to increase how high the gauge went every day. I quickly found out this was easier said then done. With my first try I barely made the gauge move more than a quarter of the way up. For the first time, I realized I couldn't take as deep a breath as I normally could. Fully understanding what I had to now accomplish with it, I kept it close to my bed at all times.

Chapter 12

Balloon Day

Later that day, when my wife, Kellee, came to visit me she entered the room with a grin and presented me with a small gift. The gift brought a huge smile to my face. Anyone who knows me knows that I am a huge Batman fan. So knowing this, my wife stopped and picked up a Batman balloon for me. The day just kept getting better. I had a new room with a view, my wife was now with me, and I had a balloon with my hero Batman on it. Things were finally starting to look better for me for the first time in a long time.

Kellee examined my new room and commented on the amazing view I now had. She was as happy as I was that I had the room to myself. I had all the privacy I wanted and also the peace and quiet I would need to get my rest.

Having been in the room for several hours now, my pain was mild. So, I sat with Kellee and talked for awhile. I showed her all my new toiletries as well as my new little breather friend, and how it worked. It seems silly to think that a lot of my conversation was about how excited I was to have the toiletries and the breathing machine, but it was all I had to talk about. My life consisted of sitting in a room by myself with hardly any outside contact or any real events happening other than nurses coming in to check on me once in awhile.

As usual, we chatted about her day and the things that went on at work. We both work at the same place, so it was somewhat necessary to keep me up-to-date on things going on. Since everyone was filling in for me while I was out, it was also necessary to ask for my help in how to handle some of my duties. We usually kept work talk short since it just seems to bring about stress which was the last thing either of us needed. Most of our other conversations consisted of funny stories about some of the odd people we constantly deal with.

During my wife's visit this time, the surgeon stopped in to check on me. He carefully examined my abdomen to make sure everything was healing properly. I was given a good bill of health and was told I should be able to eat soon. The doctor explained to me that I could not eat until my intestines started to function again. I was told that when the intestines are touched by any kind of outside force they instantly stop functioning. Since I had my abdomen cut open and half of my large intestines cut out, my intestines were in shock. He explained that in another day or so they should start to function and that I would soon be either passing gas or having bowel movements. When either one happened, it would signify that my intestines were working and I would once again be allowed to eat solid food.

Kellee stayed with me for a few more hours to keep me company and spend as much time with me as possible. As much as I had missed her, she had missed me just the same, if not more. I was told often how empty our home was without me and that she missed having me by her side as she slept. It brought great joy to my heart to feel so loved and missed. I am certain things like that helped speed up my recovery. Nothing seemed more important than keeping a positive attitude and telling myself that I would get better real soon. I had fought to stay alive for my wife, and now I was fighting to recover so that I could go home to her.

Chapter 13

I Can See Clearly Now

As the days passed, I found myself to be more appreciative of things that had previously seemed so trivial. I know it's cliché, but it really is true that when one comes close to death and recovers, it completely changes your outlook on life. You become grateful for all the small things. I never could have imagined how true that is.

Of course, I was most grateful to be alive, but with each passing day the world seemed to be more amazing than I had really noticed in the past. I found myself constantly staring out the window studying every inch of the landscape. I had always had a fondness for the outdoors, but now it seemed stronger. The trees looked more beautiful than before. The way the mountains rolled in the background seemed perfect, as if a painter himself had created a masterpiece from his own imagination. It was like I was discovering a whole new world - a world that had been right in front of me all this time, but I had never truly seen it. Going through this experience changed my view of the world. I started to feel like an explorer discovering a new world - seeing amazing, fantastic sights that no one had ever witnessed before.

Most importantly, my love for my wife had grown ever stronger. She had always meant the world to me, but now she had been by my side day after day taking care of me and showing me just how much I meant to her, I was more in love with her than ever before. She did everything in her power to take care of me day in and day out. I will never be able to describe to her how much I appreciated everything she did for me.

Understandably, this took a huge toll on my wife, just as it would with anyone in her situation. It is extremely painful to watch someone you love suffer. It makes you feel so helpless that you can't cure them and make the pain go away. It pained me as I watched the stress push my wife to the limits on a daily basis. Kellee is a very strong person. If she wasn't so strong, I'm sure she would have had a breakdown or something.

I did what I could to help her through it all. No matter how sick I was, I was never too sick to care for my wife. She constantly yelled at me for doing so, since I was the sick one in need of care. She was supposed to be taking care of me, not vice versa. I had to constantly remind her that no matter what, I would always be there for her and do whatever I could within my power to care for her.

When you find someone you love, someone that means more to you than anything else, you will do anything for them. No matter what obstacle may be put in your way, you push through and give it all that you can. No matter what may come, I will always be there for my wife, and I will never stop trying to make her happy. I will make sure that she always knows that I love her and that I did it all for her.

Chapter 14

Feast Fit For A King

I awoke the next morning feeling better than I had in a long time. I was finally starting to get some solid sleep since the pain from my surgery had been decreasing with each passing day. I no longer had the pain in my abdomen from the tumor, my incision was healing nicely, and finally overall I was getting better.

I spent the first part of my day relaxing, watching TV, and working with my lung exerciser periodically. About mid-morning I noticed a familiar feeling in my lower abdomen that I hadn't had in what seemed like forever. My intestines had kicked into gear and started working again. I felt both relived and scarred at the same time. It meant they were healing as they should but now I would be facing my first bowel movement since the surgery. I was unaware of what to expect, all I knew was that my doctor had told me it might be painful the first time after the surgery and to be prepared.

I was now faced with the daunting task of getting out of bed and making my way to the bathroom. I took my time getting to the edge of the bed. I wanted to give myself as much time as I could to prepare for what might happen. I could have called a nurse to help me but I figured my legs were feeling stronger and I had to start walking on my own sooner or later.

I took a deep breath and slowly pushed myself off the edge of the bed until my feet touched the ground. My red hospital socks with white, wavy gripping lines stopped me from sliding and falling. I held on tightly to the bed and started to stand. To my relief, my legs held steady. I pushed myself up the rest of the way and proceeded to take my first step. Though I could only move my feet a few inches at a time, I was finally walking on my own.

I never felt more like an old man than I did now. Although I was only 29, I felt as if I was 89. I could barely move my legs to walk. I was hunched over and unable to stand up straight with out pulling on the staples in my abdomen. The distance to the bathroom though only a few feet seemed like a mile. Regardless of the difficulty, I pushed on and eventually made it to my destination.

Pulling my hospital gown up I slowly lowered myself down onto the toilet with the help of the grab bars on the walls to hold me steady. Once down, things began to happen, it was painful as I was warned, but painful in a way I had not experience before. Since half of my large intestines had been removed, my small intestines had to be moved over to meet up with the part of my large intestines that still remained. The best way to describe the type of pain is that it felt like really bad cramps - almost as if someone's hand was in there squeezing and pulling on the organs inside my body.

At first I was shocked to see what had come out of me. I looked into the toilet after I had stood up and saw that it was filled with blood. My first reaction was total fear, but then my logical thinking kicked in and I realized that what I was seeing was just blood from the surgery. After they sealed me up, blood from the surgery had pooled in my intestines and was now making its way out. I felt fine, so I wasn't too worried. As the day went on I visited the bathroom again and there was less blood than before. My logic had proven right, and as far as I was concerned I felt fine and I was okay.

Later in the day around lunch time my doctor came to visit and check up on me. He examined my incision and removed the tapped bandages completely since they were no longer needed. This was the first time I was able to actually see the entirety of my incision. I was amazed at how long it was and fascinated by the amount of staples that were protruding from my stomach.

After his examination he asked how I was doing and if anything new had developed. I told him that I had my first bowel movement and despite being painful everything went okay. He was very happy to hear that since it meant I was doing well and was way ahead of schedule with healing. He and the nurses had been fairly surprised at how fast I was recovering from the surgery. I was doing better then most of the people they normally treat because most people who have colon cancer are older.

As good as that news was, what my doctor told me next was the best thing I had heard in a lifetime. Since my bowels were functioning again, I could now finally after over a week with out sustenance eat solid food again. Never before had the thought of a meal made me so happy. As the doctor left, he said he would send someone by with lunch.

I was grinning from ear to ear. I was so excited that I didn't care what it was, and I certainly didn't care that it was going to be crappy hospital food. None of that mattered in the slightest bit. After about a half hour there was a knock at the door and a hospital aide showed up with a tray of food for me. I propped myself up, pulled my bed tray over and awaited my feast.

As the aide placed it on the table for me I got my first whiff of food that I was actually going to be able to eat. It tickled the inside my nose and made my tongue salivate. The scent, whatever it was, was pure intoxication to my senses. As the aide left, I removed the top and saw the most beautiful sight ever. Since I had begun my fasting, I craved a hamburger more than anything. It was all I thought about and all I wanted. Now my dream had come true! Underneath the cover was a hamburger waiting for me! It was all mine, and no one was there to tell me I couldn't have it. I no longer had to suffer.

I noticed it had a lot of onions on it and I hate onions, but I didn't care. I scraped them off and devoured the hamburger. To anyone else it was just a crappy hospital burger, but to me it was a feast. I reveled in the taste as if it was the greatest tasting hamburger I had ever eaten.

I finished the hamburger in less than a minute, and then searched my tray for the other goodies they had brought me. I found a single serving pudding and a small soda. I tore into the package of the pudding and grabbed my glorious plastic spoon and dove into the cup. Lifting the spoon to my mouth my tongue again began to salivate like a waterfall. I slipped the spoon into my mouth and gave a small sigh of utter enjoyment, never had vanilla pudding tasted so good. I shoveled spoonful after spoonful into my mouth until I scraped the plastic container clean of every last drop.

Happy and content with my meal, I sat back and sipped on my soda with a smile on my face. I had a full belly and I was the happiest man alive. My fasting had ended and I was finally satisfied.

From then on, the next few days in the hospital were a lot easier to cope with. I was able to eat, I had an excellent view, and I received visitors on a daily basis which helped immensely to relieve my boredom. One of the biggest surprise visits was a friend by the name of Tony. He had been a customer for years at where I worked, and most times when he would stop in we would talk for awhile. Conversations ranged from topics of cars, to his many travels around the globe, and everything in between.

Over time I had gotten to know him fairly well and he spoke of his sister who in the past had dealt with her own cancer battle. Knowing what it's like to see a family member struggle with such a battle since my own mother had done so, I asked often how his sister was doing and to my pleasant surprise she was always well. In any other situation I would find it very odd that a customer of mine would want to visit me while in the hospital, but I suppose since he was very familiar with my condition and what I was going through it probably hit him a little closer to home.

So after I had been in my own room for a day or so, he made a special trip to come and see me and check on how I was doing. It was great to see a familiar yet new face for a change. We talked for some time about how I was doing and when I would be back at home and work. It really changed my perspective about people. I'd spent most of my life assuming that outside of my own family, most people didn't really care that much about me. Now here was a man that I had only known a few short years through small conversations, and he came to the hospital to spend some time with me and see how I was. It's kind gestures like that which I will never forget.

Chapter 15

Healing

Now that I could finally eat, my strength was beginning to come back. Thanks to this, I was able to get myself in and out of bed when I wanted and walk around to try and get my full mobility back. Most of my time was spent walking over to the window where I would stand clutching my hospital gown and just day dreaming about gaining my freedom back.

I still couldn't walk at a normal pace nor stand up straight, but the fact that I could get around when I wanted or needed to was a much welcomed change. Laying in bed day in and day out was starting to bring about pain in new places and was becoming a nuisance. Since I could now do laps around my room this helped alleviate the problem and gave me something new to do.

I continued working with my lung exercise machine most days, it was still tough to take deep breaths but as time went on I grew stronger. My pain from the surgery lessened as well with each day, though I was still dependant on pain killers to help me cope. As each day went on, I would push myself to walk faster and stand up straighter. I had been through a lot and came out okay and it was now time to get myself strong enough to finally go home.

My doctors routinely checked in on me and watched my progress closely. Being that I was so young, I was healing quickly. This made everyone, especially my wife and I, extremely happy. Most people that have colon cancer and have to go through the same surgery as me were well into their 50's or older, and their bodies don't heal as fast. Since I was young, strong, and healthy, my body was able to bounce back much quicker than the other patients that they normally deal with.

I spent about three to four days in my room at the hospital, and with each passing day I grew stronger and healthier and finally I received the news I had been waiting for. Early in the morning my doctor came in to check on my progress and with a smile he said "Well it looks like you may be able to go home today." It was great news, but I was still a little weary of taking the next step. So with a little hesitation I told him I would feel a bit more comfortable to give it one more night just to be sure. He told me that would be fine and that he would set up my discharge for the following day.

Later that day when my wife arrived to visit I told her of the good news. A huge smile came to her face and she told me how excited and happy she was to hear this and gave me a long, much needed hug. Seeing as how I would be leaving, Kellee asked me if there was any particular food I would want her to pick up for me and have waiting in the car. With a sly grin I told her to get me a big package of soft chocolate chip cookies - a favorite of mine from childhood thanks to my grandfather. Knowing how much I loved those little round pieces of sugary, chocolate heaven, my wife assured me that they would be waiting for me in the car the next day when she came to finally bring me home. With a smile on my face I leaned back into my bed and let thoughts of devouring them dance through my mind. Tomorrow would be a great day.

Chapter 16

Going Home

I woke the next morning feeling good about life. One of the worst things I had ever experienced was now about to take a positive turn. Though I still had several weeks of healing ahead of me, the thought of being home - someplace familiar, someplace safe -made it all seem okay.

My wife would not be there to pick me up until sometime in the afternoon, so I had to wait it out and do what I could to make the time pass. I had my breakfast, did my laps, stood at my window day dreaming, doing everything I could to make the time go by quicker. Of course since I was eager to leave, the day dragged on forever. Nothing seemed to make the day pass any faster.

Around lunch time, my doctor stopped in to check on me one more time. Both of us were satisfied with my condition and it was agreed that I was finally ready to leave. My discharge papers were signed, I received my prescription papers, and said goodbye to my doctor.

The next few hours went even more slowly than the first half of the day. I spent most of the time watching TV trying to keep my mind off of going home. I was eager to leave. I was so excited to finally be in my own home, in my own bed. I couldn't wait to be around familiar surroundings, it seemed like I had been in the hospital for months, when in reality it had been less than a week.

Finally the afternoon had come, I heard a faint knock on the door and my wife entered with a beautiful smile on her face. I could tell she was even more excited than me that I was going to finally fill the void at home. Her husband was finally going to be at her side once again.

She brought clothes for me to dress in and a few plastic bags to pack my things in. Much like most people do at hotels, we packed up every toiletry they had supplied me with to take home. Why let them go to waste? I could continue to use them while I healed at home.

Once I was dressed, Kellee went to get one of the nurses to get me on my way. She came back with a nurse who was pushing a wheelchair. I was very happy to see the wheelchair. The thought of walking all the way to the other end of the hospital to get to the car seemed like an impossible task. With their help, I eased into the chair and prepared for my journey.

We made our way past the nurses' station where I waved goodbye and thanked them for everything they had done. We pushed on down the hall into the elevator and made our descent. The closer we got to the entrance of the hospital, the more excited I became. Finally at the front door I could see day light again. I could see freedom. The doors opened and a warm, soft breeze entered. It pushed against my face and felt like a dream. The moment I was outside, I took as deep a breath as I could and reveled in my first taste of fresh air in what seemed like an eternity.

Kellee left the nurse and me at the curb as she went to get the car. When it came around she got out and opened the passenger door. I looked inside and sure enough there was my package of soft chocolate chip cookies waiting for me. Moving them aside, they both helped me climb out of the chair and into the passenger seat. It was a lot harder and more painful than I had anticipated, but with some grunts and groans and familiar pain I made it in and buckled my seatbelt. I waived my final farewell to the nurse and we set off for home.

As soon as we started moving I opened the window and let the sweet, fresh air in that I had so missed. I stuck my hand out the window feeling the air moving over my skin. The feel and the smell of it was intoxicating. Only one thing could make this moment better - I reached over and grabbed my package of cookies. I tore it open and took in a deep breath as the smell hit my nose. I grabbed a cookie and took a bite tantalizing my taste buds. It was the best thing they had encountered in weeks. I was once again in heaven, fresh air, sunshine, cookies, and I was on my way home.

Chapter 17

Home At Last

During the rest of the car ride, I found myself once again staring out the window noticing just how beautiful the world is. We passed by a small lake that was glistening from the sun. The rays of sunshine danced and swayed all over the surface, it was like witnessing natures own ballet. The water though normally a murky brown, seemed a brilliant dark shade of blue as it reflected off the sky. It was breathtaking.

As the ride went on, we passed more beautiful views of the rolling hills and countryside. It was too early in the year for the trees to be green, but the hills filled with grass took over the job of teasing my eyes with pleasantries. There seemed to be no shortage of wondrous sights as we made our way home. With each turn something new popped out and caught my eyes. It was like being born all over again - everything seemed new and bright and enchanting.

I found myself once again falling into the same cliché. Having experienced my own near-death experience, everything in the world was now more beautiful than ever. I reached over to my wife and gently caressed her arm. She smiled at me, to which I responded back with my own smile. I wanted so much to share with her my new view of the world, but alas I didn't think she could fully understand. The fact that she was there to share it with me, though only I could see it, made an even bigger impression on me. I was with the woman who meant the world to me as I was discovering a beauty I had never seen before.

Throughout the car ride, I had found many amazing sights to dazzle my eyes with, but the greatest sight to see was yet to come. At last we made the turn into our driveway, and I was finally home. We were greeted in the drive way by my mother in law who was waiting to help me out of the car and up the stairs to our apartment. With some grunting and groaning I managed to get out of the car and slowly walk towards the steps. Although I was offered help to get up the stairs, I declined. It was important to me that I do it on my own. Grabbing onto the rail I pulled myself slowly up the stairs. One step at a time I made my way to the last part of my journey.

At home I was greeted by flowers and cards from my wife's parents wishing me well and welcoming me back. Some of the furniture had been rearranged to make it easier for me to get around, since my mobility was still limited and would be for some time. Slowly step by step, I made my way to the couch where I plopped down to rest. I was feeling good, but I was still short on strength and stamina. The climb had taken quite a bit out of me.

Sitting on the couch I munched away at the cookies that my wife had brought me. Both she and her mother ran around the whole apartment getting things set up for me as they explained how they cleaned the entire place from top to bottom for my own safety from germs and possible infections. I hadn't really thought about that prior to their mentioning it. Although it was a real risk, at that moment I didn't care. I was home, I was eating something delicious, and I was content.

As evening drew near, we both sat and watched TV together. I could tell Kellee was the happiest she had been in a long time. I was finally home and she no longer had to spend her evenings alone. I myself was just as happy to be home. I could relax and just enjoy the moment.

Later in the evening, we started to get things ready for me to sleep. Since I couldn't yet lay all the way flat nor stand up totally straight it was decided it might be easier for me to sleep on the fold out couch bed. That way I could prop myself up against the back and hopefully be more comfortable. So we pulled out the bed and Kellee began to dress it with sheets and blankets.

As she was doing so, a new mild pain started to form in my abdomen. At first I didn't think much of it since I had been in constant pain since my surgery as my body tried to heal. The pain began to increase fairly quickly and soon started to worry both my wife and I. Since I had been released from the hospital ahead of schedule we began to worry if we had left too soon and that something serious might be wrong. I began to pace back and forth around the living room hoping that the pain would go away on its own and that it was just some fluke cramp. The aching pain seemed to only get worse and made me start to panic which seemed to increase the pain. We started to wonder if I might have to be rushed to the emergency room to be looked over. The biggest fear was that perhaps my intestines had become twisted or pinched in some sort of way, and that they might have to cut me open once again.

Of course, that was the last thing either of us wanted. I had just returned home and now I may have to go back to the hospital and do it all over again. Kellee did what she could to calm me down, but I could tell she was just as worried as I was and totally exhausted. I continued to pace back and forth for a while trying to decide what to do. After some time I sat down at the edge of the freshly made bed and took a few deep breaths to try and calm myself. I gently rubbed around the area where the pain was in hopes of finding some way to subdue it. To my astonishment, it seemed to work. The pain slowly began to decrease, and we both shared a great sigh of relief that I appeared to be okay. Once the pain went away, we waited for awhile before going to bed to make sure that it would stay gone. We watched some more TV till we were both satisfied that I was okay to spend the night at home.

With the help of my wife I was once again pulling and tugging and being pushed into place on the bed. As it turned out the couch bed was very hard to get in and out of because of my limited mobility. I was starting to think it was a bad idea to spend the night there, but since it had taken so much effort to get me into place I chose to stay.

Once I was settled in, Kellee turned out the lights and went into our bedroom to sleep. I had a feeling I wouldn't see much sleep that night and I was right. I spent most of the time moving around the bed trying to get myself comfortable but no matter what I did I was still in pain. Sometime during the middle of the night during all my tossing and turning, I found myself in need of the bathroom. Not wanting to wake my wife I decided to try and get out of the bed on my own. A task that I would soon find out would be more difficult than I could have imagined.

Getting in and out of the hospital bed was extremely easy compared to where I was now. I had the help of having bars on the side of the bed to grab onto to help me pull myself up and steady me as I made my way to my feet. Now however, I had no bars to grab onto. I had to find a way to get myself up and out. At first I tried to sit up, but that soon became painfully clear that it was not going to happen. I laid there for a moment trying to figure out how on earth I was going to do this. The only conclusion I could come up with was to try to roll myself onto my side then push myself up.

I started to try to roll myself over. I rocked back and forth much like a turtle does when it's stuck on its back. It probably would have been an amusing sight to see. I continued until I finally made it to my side, which unfortunately turned out to be an extremely painful position. I could feel the pressure pulling on the staples in my abdomen. I had gotten this far, I had to keep going. I took a small breath and pushed myself up to a seated position. I slowly slid myself to the side of the bed and finally managed to get myself up on my feet. I must have made more noise than I thought and woken up my wife during my struggle. As I started to walk I heard her faint voice call out from the bedroom to ask if I was alright. Despite being in pain, I assured her I was fine and went into the bathroom.

Getting back into the bed turned out to be just as difficult as getting out, but with some time and effort and more pain I finally made it and once again tried to settle in and get some rest. I tossed and turned the rest of the night, never getting more than a half hour of sleep at a time. Although I didn't sleep much that night, it was still better than the nights before my surgery where I was not only in pain but also fearing for my life. Now all I had to worry about was finding the least painful position to lie in.

Chapter 18

Day One

As the morning light started to creep in through the windows, my wife soon woke to get ready for work. She helped me out of bed and put the couch back together for me so that I could sit and relax while she made breakfast. After having my surgery I was advised by the doctors to keep a very low fiber diet which would put less strain on my intestines and give them a chance to heal. So, every morning I began eating eggs with either bacon or sausage. This was fine with me since I love both bacon and sausage.

It was harder than I had imagined to stick to a low fiber diet. There is so much hype about eating more fiber, but more foods have fiber in them than you'd think. We had to spend a lot of time reading labels and planning meals. However, after all we had been through, this seemed easy. I had to spend at least 2 weeks on the extreme low fiber diet, and then I could slowly start adding fiber back. I was told that it would take about 6-8 weeks for my body to heal enough before I could return completely to my regular diet.

In about a month, once I was strong enough, I would have to have another surgery to implant a port into my chest for my upcoming chemotherapy treatments. Even though they had removed the tumor and all the other infected body tissue from me, I would still have to receive chemotherapy as a precaution to eradicate any and all traces of cancer cells within me.

Since there wasn't much I could do in the form of physical activity, I spent most days catching up on daytime television again. I continued to do laps around my home throughout the day to get a little exercise which would help me heal faster. It also helped to relieve some of the boredom and cabin fever that was settling in. I started taking trips with my wife to the grocery store just to get out of the house for a little while. It wasn't the most exciting activity in the world but it was an escape from the walls that were starting to make me crazy.

I grew stronger with each passing day. I was able to stand up straighter and get around easier. Some days I would push myself harder than others in an effort to see how much I could do. Some days were better than others. Sometimes I would push myself too hard and pay for it later, but I knew that in the end it would be worth it.

I would soon face a challenging trip from my home in Connecticut to Pittsburgh, Pennsylvania to attend a wedding. It was very much undecided after my surgery if we would even be able to make the trip. It really all came down to how quickly I could heal and if I would be strong enough to endure the trip. Although I could get around easier, it was still difficult for me to get in and out of cars and sit in the same position for extended periods of time.

Some would wonder why I would push myself that hard just to attend a wedding. I knew my wife really wanted to go. The bride's parents were relatives and good friends. They had moved away and we had not seen them in a long time. My wife had a strong emotional tie with them and it broke her heart when they left. Since I love my wife and her happiness means more to me than anything, I agreed to make the trip no matter how tough it might be on me. I also knew it would mean a lot to the bride's parents if we could make it. I knew they would understand if we could not and life would go on, but I missed them a lot and wanted to make them happy.

So we made the arrangements and told them that we would be making the trip after all. To say that everyone was happy and excited would be a huge understatement. Even though it would be a long hard trip, I was glad to be going.

Chapter 19

On The Road Again

The morning of our trip I made sure to carry my pain meds with me rather than pack them away in my suitcase. I knew with the length of this trip I was going to need to have them handy at all times. I knew the terrain well since I had lived in Pennsylvania for much of my life, and as any local knows, the roads aren't the best. The harsh winters and heavy traffic really take their toll on the highways and create quite a rough ride in a lot of spots.

We talked about how great it was going to be to see everyone again as we glided over the rolling hills in Connecticut. I spent most of my time enjoying the scenery as I listened to my wife and her parents discuss the wedding. Up until this day I hadn't traveled much farther than the local grocery store in town, so it was a much welcomed change to be able to be out and seeing the world again.

As predicted, when we reached Pennsylvania the roads became rough. We hit pothole after pothole some with shoddy patchwork to fill them in. The car shook and bounced like an off road vehicle. My wife did her best to avoid them but there were so many at times it was impossible. I was very glad at that moment that I had taken my meds before we left. I was still in pain but I knew it would have been much worse had I waited.

Thankfully the roads weren't that way for the whole trip, the farther into Pennsylvania we traveled, the better the roads became. After some time the forests parted ways and we were able to finally gain access to some of the amazing views Pennsylvania has to offer. Most of Pennsylvania is filled with mountains so the roads we traveled on curved up and down and all around, this gave us amazing mountain top views as well as picturesque valleys.

The beautiful sites alone were enough to keep me distracted from the pain I was incurring from not only the rough roads but having sat so long in a fixed position. My abdomen was still weeks away from fully healing, so with every bump and jolt the seatbelt dug into me tugging at my incision. As unpleasant as it was I was still happy that I wasn't stuck at home going crazy anymore. I was with my loving wife and her parents, viewing the beautiful countryside of America on my way to see people we all dearly cared about.

Throughout the trip we made a few pit stops for both food and restroom breaks. Each time I exited or entered the car I was reminded of just how much lost mobility I still had. I began to joke with Kellee and her parents that I now matched her fathers pace. He himself has a lot of trouble getting in and out of vehicles and just walking in general. His issues come from being a hard worker his whole life and often pushing his body to the limits, after many years of abuse it really took its toll on him.

Despite having trouble getting around, he never lets it stop him. He is without a doubt one of the most determined individuals it has been my pleasure to know in life. He often reminds me a lot of my father, and my grandfather who had passed away. They all come from generations of people who didn't know the meaning of the word quit, they work hard and earn the things they have in life. They aren't anything like my generation or those younger than me who feel that the world owes them everything for nothing. Knowing my father in law the way I do, I know for sure that just like my own grandfather, he will never stop working or trying until the day he dies. I have the utmost respect for him because of that. All of us who know him try as hard as we can to make him slow down and take it easy but he never listens, and I know he never will.

After about 10 hours of constant driving we finally reached Pittsburgh and found our hotel. I went inside to check in while everyone else unpacked the car and to my surprise I was greeted by the parents of the bride Bud and Lisa. When they saw me they both did a double take to make sure that they did in fact see me, after realizing it was me I was welcomed with warm smiles and gentle hugs.

Oddly enough, it ended up being a somewhat awkward moment for me, since I had lost so much weight most of my clothes were now hanging off of me, and with out the help of a belt my pants would have fallen down. During the last few hours of the drive I had to loosen my belt to keep it from digging into my incision. Having forgotten about that when I entered the hotel my pants nearly fell down as I walked, after a few steps I started to feel my pants slide down, luckily I was quick enough to grab onto them. So there I was hugging friends and relatives with one hand and using the other to hold up my pants and spare myself the embarrassment of showing the world my underpants.

No one made mention of me hand holding my pants, and in my hunched over position I guess most of them thought I was just in pain and holding my stomach, which in a sense was somewhat true. Had they known the truth, I am sure they would all have had a good laugh. We talked a little and they thanked me several times for coming, knowing how much effort it took just to be there. It made me happy to know that not only did I make them happy, but knowing they cared and worried about me put a special warm feeling in my heart.

By now running into people I know and having them ask me a million times how I was doing and telling me that I looked great had become such a routine that most conversations were just put into autopilot. I was always asked the same things from everyone so I just automatically responded with the same answers time and time again. After awhile it started to somewhat become annoying, but I really didn't mind, I knew it just meant that they cared. It was the fact of knowing that I had so many people that cared about me kept me going and made me want to fight to get better.

As the day went on I ran into more friends and family that all had come for the wedding, the same routine continued as before until finally all curiosity had been satisfied. After finally finding a moment to excuse our selves we went to our hotel room to get settled and made plans to have dinner with Kellee's parents and her uncle Joe. By now I was exhausted, I had used up a lot of my energy during the long car ride so a nice relaxing dinner sounded like a fantastic idea. To make it through the night I popped a few more pills to ease my pain and settled in to watch some TV and take it easy while Kellee went off to organize our dinner plans.

To make sure I didn't fall asleep while she was gone I began to unpack some things and make sure my tux had survived the trip, more importantly I had to make sure the shoes I had packed survived. Since I had two weddings that year to attend (one prior to this one), and unbeknownst to everyone out side of my wife and her parents I decided to buy a special pair of black and white wingtip dress shoes. I wanted to add a little pizzazz to the events and give everyone something to smile at and hopefully keep their minds on happier things other than my illness. They ended up having more of an effect at the weddings than I had predicted.

Later on that evening my wife and I and her parents met up with her uncle in the lobby and headed into one of the hotels restaurants. The evening went well, I had enough energy to make it through and be cheery. As Kellee's father always says, we were making memories. We ate, drank, told stories, and just had a very pleasant evening. Since all of us were tired from the journey we called it quits fairly early, tomorrow after all was the big day and we needed to be well rested for a long day of celebration.

Chapter 20

Wedding Bells

Luckily for me I had slept great through the night. When I woke, I felt better than I had for many days. This was a welcomed sign that I would be able to make it through the long day. I would soon find out the day was going to be much longer than I had anticipated.

We had a nice leisurely breakfast that morning, trying to keep things easy for me and save my energy for later. We discussed the plans for the day to get our schedule straight and make everything run as smooth as possible. We finished our breakfast and headed back to the hotel room to start getting dressed for the wedding. I cleaned lint off my tux while my wife put on her makeup. We both danced around each other running after things we needed to get ready.

Knowing how much weight I had lost and that I hadn't worn my tux since my own wedding four years prior, we planned ahead and I borrowed suspenders from her father to help prevent a repeat of events like what happened in the hotel lobby. The last thing anyone needed to see was me dancing with my wife and have my pants fall down. Although it would have made a good laugh and perhaps a video with a chance to win $10,000 on TV, I was not ready to show the world my unmentionables.

Finally dressed, we grabbed everything we would need for the evening and headed off to meet up with everyone else to catch the limo to the church. My shoes were shiny and ready for their debut. From the moment I stepped out of the hotel room, my shoes instantly caught the attention of all passerby's'. Even complete strangers were commenting on them.

We met up with Kellee's parents in the hallway and caught the elevator down to the lobby. Her parents, being old-fashioned, loved my shoes. Not too many people wear retro style shoes like them anymore, so they were pleased to see them and reminisce about the past. So far my plan was working. The shoes made people smile and kept their minds on happier thoughts, and it in turn kept my own mind on something other than my pain. Once in the lobby, we were greeted by other guests who were also waiting for the limo. Once again all eyes fell on my shoes and the comments began to fly. Everyone liked them and talked about them, and for once they all forgot about the troubles that were plaguing me.

After a few moments of mingling, the limo arrived and we all piled in to make our way to the church. Climbing in and out of the limo once again reminded me of how hard it was to get around, especially since I had to make my way several feet up towards the front to make room for all the other guests, but I managed. I wasn't going to let my pain get the best of me after how far I had come.

We arrived at the church in just a few minutes and once again I had to crawl my way out of the limo, grunting and groaning I struggled but eventually I was free. We said our hellos to the other guests as we proceeded into the church to find a place to sit. We found a nice quiet place to our elves and commented on the amazing architecture of the building. I had been in several churches in my life but never a cathedral. The amount of work and effort that went into the building was astonishing.

The ceremony itself was beautiful. Everything went according to plan, no one passed out, and everyone was happy. After the ceremony, it was time to once again finagle myself into the limo for another ride, this time we were headed to Carnegie Music Hall for the reception. Knowing what to expect, getting into the limo was easier this time as was getting out when we arrived.

We spent the cocktail hour mingling again with the other guests, and as predicted my shoes were a hit. Many people that had not seen them earlier were now coming up to me to compliment me on them. Even the servers liked them and made sure to tell me. I couldn't have planned it better.

We had a great time at the reception. Everyone was happy and having fun - dancing, eating, and sharing old memories. The bride's parents made a special point of once more telling me how grateful they were that I had been able to make the trip. Though I had only known them for a few short years, they welcomed me into the family with loving arms and made sure that I knew it. I had always felt kind of like an outcast in life. I never really thought that I made an impression on people. With the exception of my own family, I never thought people really cared about me. It was moments like that night that helped to change my view on life and people.

The night soon drew to an end, for us at least. My energy was wearing thin and my feet were killing me. My new shoes were pretty to look at, but were also the most painful footwear I had ever worn. Kellee took great enjoyment out of the joke that I finally knew what it was like to be a woman. Tired and my feet throbbing, we said our goodbyes since we were not sure if we would see any of them again in the morning before we left. We then made our way back to the hotel room. As soon as we reached our room, I changed into my pajamas and collapsed into the bed. I was asleep as soon as my head hit the pillow.

The trip home was much like the trip down - long and hard, but we made it. We unpacked our bags, and since it was late we went straight to bed. We had a long fun weekend, but we were exhausted and sleep was the only thing on both of our minds.

Chapter 21

Emergency Room

A few weeks had passed since the wedding. I had more time to recuperate and gain my strength back for my next surgery. Since I was soon going to be doing chemotherapy, I had to have a surgery to have a port implanted into my chest. The port would be placed just under the skin with a line that went directly to the main artery of my heart. Even though it was going to be a small quick surgery lasting no more then twenty to thirty minutes, I was dreading having it done. The thought of having this thing in my chest and being able to see and feel it under my skin was not appealing to me. It sent shivers down my spine and I wanted more than anything to avoid it. However, since it was necessary, I had no choice. I knew deep down that despite the discomfort of having the implant, it was going to save my life.

Before the surgery I met with a new doctor, the oncologist, who was going to care for me and examine me during my chemo treatments. He looked over my tests and explained to me that I was going to have a total of twelve chemotherapy treatments over twenty-four weeks. I was to receive a treatment over the course of three days then be given a week and a half to recuperate before the next treatment was to be given. Although they had removed the tumor and any traces of cancer they could find, I would still need the treatments as a precaution to kill off any unseen cancer cells that might still exist.

During my first visit with the doctor, I was given some very unpleasant news. It looked very positive that I would beat cancer this time, but I was informed that since I was so young and had developed colon cancer, I would be at high risk for getting some form of cancer or another at some point again in my life. My life expectancy rate had dropped dramatically. Basically what the doctor was telling me was that I would be lucky to reach old age. Though he had seen cases were people were like me and developed cancer this early and lived long and healthy lives with out it returning, it was not likely.

I was once again faced with my own mortality. It's enough to make anyone depressed or even drive them crazy. From that moment on, not a single day goes by that I don't think about it. It's like having a death sentence hanging over my head, but I have not, nor will I ever give up in my fight.

After meeting with the doctor, he had one of the nurses who actually does the treatments come into the examining room to explain the whole procedure and show me what the actual port looks like that would be implanted in my chest. After having seen what would actually be put into my chest I was even less enthusiastic about having it done. Once again, chills went down my spine and an uneasy feeling entered my stomach.

We made arrangements for the surgery and in about two weeks I was once again going to be going under the knife. I took those two weeks to gather my thoughts and do my best to be ready for another operation. The days went by and I started to feel confident about the surgery. Knowing that it would be nowhere near as invasive as the previous surgery had helped put my mind at ease.

The day before my surgery was like any other - I woke up, showered, and got dressed. I spent most of the day relaxing at home and doing little things to keep myself busy. However as the afternoon approached I started to feel a new pain in my abdomen It had been eight weeks since my surgery and I hadn't had abdominal pain in some time. It started out as a very mild discomfort but as time went on it got worse. Kellee soon came home from work and I told her what was going on. She seemed more worried than I at first and asked if I wanted to go to the emergency room. Thinking it would pass I told her no and decided to lie on the couch for a bit to see if it would pass while she made dinner.

The Crappiest Year Ever

While she busied herself with dinner, I laid on the couch clenching my stomach. The pain was getting worse with each passing minute. Nothing I did could make it go away. Fears started running through both of our heads. What if something had torn open or if my intestines wrapped them selves in a knot?

Approximately a half hour had passed and I finally decided it was time to go to the emergency room. It took me forever to get dressed. I was in so much pain I could barely stand. I had to hold myself up against my dresser in order to pull my pants up with my other hand. Although only a few minutes, it seemed like it took hours for me to get dressed and make my way to the car.

A half hour later and some high-speed driving, Kellee and I arrived at the hospital. I slowly made my way to the receptionist's desk and began to tell her what was wrong. By this time I was in so much pain I was using both arms to grip on to the counter to stay on my feet. Seeing the urgency of my condition they rushed me into an examining room. I figured with the amount of pain I was in a doctor would be in right away to see me, once again I was proven wrong.

I lay on the examining table for about twenty minutes clenching my stomach, moaning as I rocked back and forth in excruciating pain. Occasionally my eyes would meet with my wife's and I could see how worried she was. Knowing how worried she gets, I tried to assure her I would be okay. When the doctor finally came in we explained my previous surgery and my pain. He decided I would need to have a CAT scan done to see what, if anything, was going on inside me.

In the meantime, he sent in a nurse to give me a shot of pain medicine to help. When she came in she told us that what they were about to give me was ten times stronger than morphine, and to be prepared that it might make me loopy. She gave me the shot and said she would be in to check on me in a little while. In the mean time I was to drink an orange flavored radioactive dye to prep for the CAT scan.

Kellee stood by my side and comforted me while I sipped away at that awful orange drink and waited for relief to come from the shot. To my dismay the shot did almost nothing, some of the pain had diminished but not much. I continued to groan in agony until the nurse returned. To her surprise I was still in pain so she decided to give me another dose of the pain meds. Finally, after a few minutes, relief had come. The medicine kicked in and the pain started to subside. By this time I was being taken in a wheelchair to have the CAT scan done.

They hooked up an IV line to my arm and pumped me full of more radioactive dye and put me into the machine. Back in the ER room, we awaited the results. By now the medicine had kicked in full gear and the pain was nearly gone. Finally, I was starting to relax and prepare myself for bad news. To our relief, the findings came up normal. They compared my CAT scan with a previous one from a few weeks ago and found that everything was normal. The doctor had no idea what was wrong with me other than to say it was just really bad cramps, from what though they had no real explanation. Perhaps something I ate, or stress, or who knows what else.

Having just been through such an ordeal, we asked if it was still wise to have the surgery the next day. The doctor told us to sit and relax while he contacted the surgeon to see what he thought. By now it was midnight, so we figured it might take some time to get an answer. After waiting for quite some time he was finally able to reach the surgeon and told us that the procedure would go on as scheduled the next day.

We made our way back to the car after thanking everyone for their help and then headed home. The drive home was very quiet, I knew my wife was exhausted and worried and stressing over me, so I reached over to hold her hand and console her. Though I was the one going through all the pain and suffering I knew it was hurting her emotionally and mentally just as much.

By the time we got home it was near one in the morning. We entered our apartment, changed into our pajamas, and went straight to bed. Tomorrow was going to be another big day which was scheduled to start very early. I had to regain as much strength and composure as possible.

Chapter 22

The Port

I woke the next morning with a similar dreadful feeling of my first surgery. Although this one was a simple non-evasive procedure, the thought of once again going under the knife was starting to stress me out. Before I knew it we were in the car and on the way to the hospital.

Upon arriving there I was greeted by familiar faces. A lot of the nurses that had cared for me during my blood transfusions and my pre-op care were there. They treated me with empathetic motherly-like care and concern. Not that I minded, it helped to put my mind at ease.

I was taken to my room where I was once again to wear one of those uncomfortable, annoying hospital gowns. After I changed, I laid in the hospital bed for some time waiting to go in for surgery. Waiting did not help with my stressful anticipation. Kellee and I talked about anything we could to try and make light of the situation and keep my mind off of what was to come. We waited about a half hour if not more before I was once again greeted by the anesthesiologist. Once more we went over the procedure and which drugs were to be used on me. I was startled to learn that I would be fully awake during the whole procedure and that they would only be using a local anesthetic to numb the area they were going to be working on. As you can imagine, this did not make me feel any better. The last thing I wanted was to be awake while they cut into me to implant something into my chest. I asked if I could be put under for the procedure but they denied me saying it wasn't necessary. I once again signed the waiver with even more dread than I had already been feeling the whole morning.

After the anesthesiologist left, the surgeon came in to see how I was and discuss the operation and the dangers of the procedure. The biggest risk of doing the implant was that there was a very small chance they could puncture one of my lungs. This was not something I wanted to hear but at least I could pretend to be prepared for the worst. I was given a basic description of what the procedure would entail from start to finish and once again told not to worry since it was a "simple procedure" and it would be over just as soon as it started.

Ten to fifteen minutes had passed before the nurse came to take me to the operating room. Kellee was allowed to escort me down to the operating room and to say goodbye to me before I went in. As the nurse entered, he looked at me and smiled and said he remembered me from last time, he jokingly said "We need to stop meeting this way." I laughed and agreed. It was a welcomed tension breaker that for a moment put me at ease. We made our way down the same hallways as last time, only this time I was left just outside of the operating room while they waited for everything to be ready. Kellee held my hand trying to calm me, and told me that she loved me and assured me that I would be okay. A few moments passed and I was wheeled into the operating room, I looked back at my wife and said I'll see you soon.

One of the things I dislike most about the operating room is how cold it is. Even though I had blankets on me, the moment you enter it's like being taken into a refrigerator. I know this is for sanitary reasons to reduce the risk of germ and bacteria growth, but it doesn't make the situation any more comforting.

Like last time, I was pushed next to the operating table and asked to slide over and lay down. I once again found it amusing to myself that it's nothing like in the movies where they lift you over. It's just another fable created by Hollywood, with the exception of those who are unconscious and cannot move themselves. I lay on the table trying to find something to focus on to keep my mind from going insane with fear. I was constantly shuffled about on the table as they placed gel packs under my back in order to make my shoulders tilt back and expose my chest more. Next, they strapped my arms and legs down to the table so I could not move.

I took slow, deep breaths to keep myself calm and keep my heart rate down. As I lay there the surgeon and nurses busied themselves making the final preparations. A needle was put into my chest to administer the anesthetic, and then they waited a few moments for it to take effect before they began. The surgeon said it was time to begin and to my relief they placed a cloth mask over my head so that I could not see what they were doing. Not that I would have looked but it was good to know that even if I wanted to, I could not witness myself being cut open.

There wasn't much I could do but just lay there and listen to what was happening. The doctors and nurses talked amongst each other as they worked. I could not seem to focus on the words that I was hearing. Everything seemed muffled and distant. It reminded me of the ambient conversations you hear in restaurants. Only a few words here and there registered with my brain, but with out hearing the whole conversation I could not put any context to what I was hearing.

For the most part I wasn't aware of anything that was going on with the procedure. This of course was a good thing; it meant that the anesthesia was doing its job. I was warned before hand that the only thing I might feel would be some pressure against my body as they pushed the implant in. Sure enough when that time came I felt the surgeon pushing down against my body as the implant was inserted and put in place. I felt no pain at all when this was done. It was just as if someone was patting me on the chest.

Before I knew it, the mask was pulled from my face and they began to release the belts that held me down. The bed I came in on was wheeled over and I was asked to slide back on to it so that I could be taken to the recovery room. Getting back onto the bed was easier said then done, I quickly found out I was already sore from the operation and my mobility was again limited. With some help, I slid myself over and was draped in blankets to bring my body temperature back up.

I sat in the recovery room for about twenty minutes while they monitored my vital signs. Once they were sure I was okay, I was taken back to my room where my wife was waiting for me. As they pushed me in I was greeted by her beautiful smile which warmed my heart. Kellee took hold of my hand and I could feel the stress just melting away.

The surgery was a complete success with no complications, and once I felt strong enough I was told I could put my clothes back on and head home to get some rest. It was going to be a few weeks before I started chemotherapy and they had to give my body time to heal. This gave me plenty of time to ready myself for the next step to my recovery and to hopefully beat cancer.

Chapter 23

Chemotherapy

The weeks after my second surgery flew by. Before I knew it I had the stitches removed and my first chemotherapy session was scheduled. When the day came, the doctor and I went over the procedure again and he gave us a chance to ask any further questions we might have before I was brought back to the treatment room.

Since it's a small doctor's office, several patients are treated at the same time in the same room. I was led to a big room in the back with reclining hospital chairs lined up one next to another in a circle around the room. When I first entered the room a feeling of despair clouded over me, I looked at the other patients who like me, were fighting for their life in a battle against cancer. Immediately I was the outcast of the group, all the other patients were elderly, ranging from late forties to somewhere in their seventies or eighties. And here I was a young healthy looking kid the age of twenty-nine. I shouldn't be here, I shouldn't have to face this battle, but I was. I was just as unfortunate as them if not more. They had lived a long and full life before being struck with this horrible disease. And here I was at the prime of my life fighting to stay a live, praying that I could one day make it to their age and live a full and complete life.

Looking around at the faces and seeing the look of what I can only describe as "being on deaths door" made my heart sink. These poor souls should be enjoying their twilight years, not fighting cancer. They should be enjoying the fruits of a long lived life and well deserved retirement. I did tried to push the horrible thoughts from my mind, but no matter where I looked there was a constant reminder of just what kind of toll cancer puts on someone. It was a bit of a reality check for me, it made me wonder if I would ever live as long as them. Even though when this all began I had prepared myself for the possibility that

The Crappiest Year Ever

I might soon die, there wasn't a chance I was just going to give up. I had come this far and survived and I would be damned if I wouldn't beat this.

With all these random, horrible thoughts dancing in my head I sat in one of the chairs to await my first treatment. I was greeted by the nurse whom we had met before as she cared for another patient. I must commend the people that work at this office. The fact that they deal with these poor souls on a daily basis and still find enough strength to be positive and care for them, is astonishing. It takes a strong person to see people suffer like this and still want to get up in the morning and face it every day. It's a nice thought to know that people like this still exist in this world and are there for people who really need someone to turn to when things are their worst.

As I waited the nurse opened some drawers next to my chair and began to pull out the supplies needed for my chemo treatment. As she pulled them out she explained what everything was used for and told me that after a few sessions I would get the full hang of it and know what to expect every time.

Once she was all set up she sprayed the area of my implant with a cold numbing spray, this was to make the insertion of the needle into my port less painful. The area was then cleaned and dried and I was ready for my first port access. I was told to take a deep breath and slowly breathe out. As I started to breathe out the needle was pushed into my chest and set in place. I winced and clamped my eyes shut. Not only did the needle itself hurt, but the area around my implant was still sore from the surgery. After a moment to let the pain die out she placed a plastic, see through, tape bandage around the port to help keep it in place in my chest.

As uncomfortable as it was I was going to have to get used to it. This needle was going to be in my chest for the next two days. While in the office they first inject me with an anti-nausea medicine then the chemo drug combination itself. This is usually about a three hour process, which if you don't have something to keep you occupied, can be a very boring and depressing time. My wife brought a book to read and I had put a bunch of episodes of Seinfeld on my phone to watch as my session went on.

Before they begin the injection process they have to flush the port first with saline solution. This was part I hated with a passion. It's not that it hurts, for the most part you feel nothing, but the saline solution for some reason always went straight to my nose and I could smell it. It's not a very pleasant smell and at times made me nauseous. The first time they flushed my port they asked if I could taste the saline. Apparently most people end up tasting it in their mouth. For me it just went straight to my nose. I guess in that sense I was lucky. The last thing I would want after smelling it would be to taste it.

They told me it was a good sign that the flush went through with out any issues. It meant that the line leading to my heart was clear and functioning properly. After the flush it was time to draw blood from my port. They hooked up vial after vial to the line to draw blood samples to test my levels. They have to make sure my red and white blood cell counts are high enough for them to safely administer the drugs. If they are too low it could be dangerous. The chemotherapy kills the caner cells, but unfortunately also kills good cells too, particularly white blood cells. This is the reason that I was given a week and a half between sessions to allow time for my body to recover.

My blood counts were spot on and it was time to begin my first treatment. Bag after bag of the drugs were pushed into my body over the three hour period. Even though I was receiving the anti-nausea drug, there was a chance that I might still tend to feel sick through the next few days while I was being treated. Since it's very common, I was given a prescription of anti-nausea pills to take as needed. Other unfortunate side effects included fatigue and diarrhea and extreme cold sensitivity all of which I would soon become too familiar with.

Once all of the other drugs have been administered, they push one more drug into my body before hooking up a pump to my port. The pump is about 4 inches wide, 8 inches tall and around 2 inches thick. The pump which my wife and I named PIA, short for "Pain In The Ass" pushes more of the chemo drug into me over a forty six hour period. This means I not only have to find a way to sleep with this thing hooked up to me, but I have to find a way to bathe with it and carry it with me every where I go. This is why we named it PIA because it became apparent very quickly just how annoying it was to have around.

After the pump was hooked up to me I was finally allowed to leave, I stood up for the first time in three hours and noticed that my legs felt achy. I figured that since I had sat for so long they had probably cramped up. However as the afternoon and night went on the pain became worse. It felt as if I had run a three hundred mile marathon and my muscles were sore and tired. It became somewhat difficult to sit still and even more difficult to get around since every muscle in my lower legs was in pain. My only saving grace was that I still had some pain meds left over from my last surgery, so before bed I took a few and tried to sleep.

Sleeping as I would find out that night was going to be difficult. That first night I had propped a pillow under my legs to try to prevent me from rolling over onto my side during the night. The last thing I wanted was to roll over too far and put pressure on the needle in my chest. I didn't sleep much that night. My legs continued to ache and I haven't really been comfortable sleeping on my back since I was a child. Up until my intestinal surgery, I hadn't slept on my back since I was in grade school. So, it was a long and dreadful night. I did manage to sleep some but not enough. I spent the next day dragging my feet around the apartment, I wasn't just tired from lack of sleep but the fatiguing side effects of the chemo were hitting me full blast.

I learned after talking to my doctor that one of the drugs affects the nerves in my body. For me it went straight to my legs and caused irritation to the nerves which was the source of my pain. Lucky for me, during my first session my side effects were pretty mild. Mostly I was just very tired. I didn't really get nauseous so I was able to eat, but to be safe I kept the food simple.

I tried to keep myself occupied through out the day to keep myself awake in hopes that when bed time came I would be tired enough to sleep through the night. That night I again placed a pillow under my legs to help keep me on my back, the aching in my legs had gone away earlier giving me one less thing to keep me from sleeping. I woke constantly through the night due to being uncomfortable, but I was able to get more sleep than the previous night which made up for it.

By the next morning I checked the level count on the pump and it was lower than I had expected, it seemed that I would be heading in earlier than the forty six hour period they plan for. As I would find out with each passing session this was to always be the case, but being the first time I wasn't sure what to do. My appointment to have the pump removed wasn't until mid day and I was almost on empty by mid morning. Worrying about what to do I called the office to ask if I could come in early, they asked if the pump had been beeping which is what it does when it gets down to a certain point, and since mine was they told me to head on down.

Kellee drove me down since it was hard to drive with the pump hooked up to me. When driving myself I not only have to find a place to put the pump where it will stay still, but being in the driver seat, the seat belt rests right over my implant making it uncomfortable. So my wife usually drove me to and from each session to make life a little easier. Kellee, being the supportive loving wife that she is, she liked to be by my side for each session to support me. Though I tell her I am fine, she worries a lot about me and insists on always being there to look after me. I don't mind. I know it comes from love and concern for my well being.

Soon enough we arrived back at the doctor's office and were led to the back room. The nurse pushed a bunch of buttons on the pump to check the level and see how much fluid was left. Since I still had a little more to go they set it up to push the last bit in much faster than the normal pace. After the last bit went in, the alarm on the pump sounded which lets you know it's empty. At this point they disconnect the pump and once again flush the line of the port. Once more I was greeted with the familiar nauseating smell of saline solution filling my nose. Just like last time, I made a sickened face and forced air out of my nose as if I was cleaning it with a tissue to help get the smell out faster.

After a few flushes with the saline they inject me with one last drug which is an anticoagulant to insure that the line that goes to my heart does not get closed off. The last thing to do is remove the needle from the port. It started with the painful peeling of the clear plastic bandage which takes chest hairs with it. It didn't take me long to learn to shave my chest before my treatments. Then they remove the needle which hurts less than the insertion but it's still enough to make me wince a little from the pain.

My vitals are checked one last time to assure that I am okay and they ask how I have been feeling. Since this was the first time, I felt almost perfectly fine, my body took it well since it hadn't yet been weakened by the chemo. Confident everything was good I was sent home. At the end of each treatment, it was always a glorious moment to be rid of PIA and be on my way back home.

Even though I was free and the session was over, I was warned that some of the side effects might come later after the drugs have been in my system for a few days. On the way home I was starving and had my wife stop for me to grab a sandwich and when we got home I devoured it. Sadly afterwards I regretted my decision because I started to feel nauseous. I would soon find out that along with the nausea I would also experience the extreme sensitivity to cold. Since it was summer, the sensitivity to cold was the one side effect I dreaded the most. This meant no cold drinks of any kind, no cold foods like ice cream or ice pops. Especially for me who loves cold things this was pure torture. The only positive note was that the side effects usually only lasted a few days.

The cold sensitivity is different for everyone. For me the first time I felt it was when I put a cold glass up to my lips to take a drink, my lip started to tingle the moment it touched it. The next symptom which is a more common one is that when you swallow something cold, the nerves in the back of the throat cause a sensation that feels like the throat is closing off similar to when someone has an allergic reaction. However it's just a mixed signal, meaning that the throat isn't actually closing off, it just feels that way. I was told that symptom has scared a lot of patients, so now they make it a point to warn them. The next symptom that I encountered was in my hands, the moment I touched anything cold it felt as if my hands had been frostbitten in the dead of winter. All the nerves in my fingers would start to tingle and create a burning sensation. Imagine its winter and you make a snowball and instead of throwing it you hold it in your hand for a few minutes. After awhile the cold from the snow actually starts to create a painful burning feeling. That's what it was like after touching something cold for just a few seconds.

I had really been hoping that I would never experience the cold sensitivity since it was summer. As luck would have it, it turned out to be one of the most prominent symptoms that I experienced. So for every other week of the summer I was denied the salvation of cold food and drinks. Although I'm sure it was just in my head, it seemed that most of the weeks I was on chemo we also would be having the hottest weather of the summer.

Chapter 24

Precursor

My wife Kellee had been coming with me to every treatment I had thus far since I began. She always felt it necessary to be there by my side even though I constantly told her that she didn't have to be. One of those days she finally decided to take up my offer and go have some time to herself. Kellee loves horses and has been riding them and competing with them since she was eight years old. Since it was a beautiful perfect summer day out and I was going to be cooped up inside all day, she decided to go riding while I did my treatment.

My session went on as normal and when I got closer to the end of it, I called her to let her know it would soon be time to come and pick me up. I figured she might not answer since she doesn't keep her phone on her while she rides and sure enough it went to her voicemail. Shortly after I called she returned my call and told me that she had taken a rather nasty fall off her horse and that she was in a lot of pain.

My heart sank with fear and dread, she tried to assure me that she was okay and would soon be down to pick me up but I just had an unnerving feeling that it would end up being more serious than she implied. Later on when she arrived to pick me up, my suspicion had been confirmed. She was in even more pain and was having a bit of trouble getting around.

At first she did not want to go to the hospital and thought she would wait it out and see if it was necessary to go, but with my constant insistence she finally agreed to go. With PIA around my shoulder we went down the street to the emergency room.

After a physical exam, and x-ray, a CAT scan, and several hours of sitting around in the ER, it was discovered that when she had fallen she chipped a piece of bone from one of her vertebrae. It was not serious, but the doctor told her that she would be in quite a bit of pain for sometime and that she would not be able to ride her horse again for a few months. This was a huge blow to her since she enjoyed it so much and used it as a means of reducing stress each week. She became very upset upon hearing this news as did I. I knew how much she loved it and now she was going to be denied it, it looked as if my streak of bad luck was starting to reach her now. It started to have me wondering who or what would be next.

As summer pushed on I continued with my treatments and I came to learn that with each session my symptoms would often change. Some symptoms where always there but others came and went. Some weeks I would experience extremely painful diarrhea and other weeks hardly at all. My sensitivity to cold was always there but some days it was worse than others. At times I could hold cold things and be okay, and even sip cold drinks slowly. Other times I couldn't even touch anything cold for more than a second with out being in pain. It began to get a little frustrating, not just having to deal with the side effects but never really knowing which ones I would have to deal with.

During the summer as my treatments went on I spoke often with my parents, I knew my mother could relate to what I was going through since she had done it before three times in the past. She often provided me with a sympathetic ear and continued to encourage me to stay strong. I called my parents often to update them on my condition, but I was also calling constantly to check on my mom. Over the last few months while I had been receiving my chemo treatments she was in and out of the hospital on a weekly basis. She continued to experience labored breathing and had to be taken to the hospital at least once a week to have fluid drained from her chest.

It was discovered that my mother had developed cirrhosis of the liver. She was overweight, diabetic, and a former smoker. She also had all the harsh drugs they had pushed into her system during her cancer battles. All of these factors had taken a huge toll on her liver. It was to the point that it was hardly functioning at all, and the fluids that it would normally process were instead building up in her body.

To help her with this they started her on different medicines which seemed to work at first but were only intended as a temporary solution, the only way she could survive was to have a liver transplant. I conveyed this information to my brother Jay who immediately stepped forward to be a donor if he was compatible. I myself would have done the same in a heartbeat, but was not eligible because I had cancer.

Since a liver transplant was the only life saving option, my mother was set up with an appointment with another doctor to see if she would be eligible to receive a transplant. After meeting with the doctor she was told that she could in fact receive a donation, however there was a long waiting list and that actually two livers were in needed in order to do a transplant. In the meantime she was told to continue with the medicine they had her on and that all she could do was wait.

This put a huge toll on my entire family. Not a day went by that we all didn't worry about her. It was especially rough since our family had been through so much in the last six months. My grandfather passed away, my mom was in and out of the hospital constantly, and I had been diagnosed with colon cancer and had come close to dying myself. What was to soon come would be the biggest blow my family had ever endured. Something none of us were prepared for, something no one ever wants to face.

Chapter 25

An Angel Is Dying

Every year in July for our wedding anniversary my wife and I head up to a small beach town in Maine. We were married there and every year since then, we head there for vacation. We love the quiet town with an undying passion. My wife and her parents had been vacationing in that area for most of her life, and she even attended college near by. After we met and got engaged she soon introduced me to the area and I fell in love with it instantly. Without hesitation we made the decision to be married there.

We always stay at the same hotel right on the water, we go to the same stores year after year and spend as much time as possible on the beach relaxing, trying our best to forget the stress that builds up in us both all year long. Every year as we approach the month of July we start to talk and day dream about our upcoming vacation. As the date comes nearer the more anxious we get to make the trek and see the welcoming beach and stretches of small shops that bring about fond memories. This year was going to be especially enjoyed since it had been such a horrible miserable year up until then. We both wanted nothing more than to get away from everything and escape all the worries that had been plaguing us, even if for just a few days. Even one of my doctors recommended taking a vacation since I had been through so much, and who am I to ignore doctor's orders.

One small downside to this year's trip was that right before we were set to leave was the Fourth of July holiday which fell on a Monday the week before our vacation. My normal chemo treatments ran from Monday to Wednesday, but because of the holiday it meant that I would be going from Wednesday to Friday. Since we had planned our vacation for the following Sunday, I would still be exhibiting most of the side effects from that weeks treatments. That meant the first day or two would somewhat miserable for me. However given the circumstances I did not care. I wanted to get away and do my best to forget everything.

As we entered the week before our vacation fate once again stepped in to delve another blow to my family. Again the universe was coming after my family, only this time it was going to hit even closer to home and deliver one of the most painful hits my family had ever encountered. I received a message from my father telling me that my mother was in the hospital again. At first it didn't mean much since she had been in there literally every week for the last month or so, but the next line that followed in the message shook every nerve in my body and sent fear throughout every fiber of my being. The next line read "It doesn't look good, will call you later tonight." My father has never really been the type of person who sugar coats things, when he says it doesn't look good, that means to expect the worst. I could already feel absolute dread working its way through my body. The thing we had all feared the most for my mother looked to finally be coming true. I sat in my chair for some time holding my phone not knowing what to say or do. No thoughts came to me, I was lost inside myself, it was one of those shocking moments where your mind just can't comprehend the situation and leaves you there an empty shell.

After a few moments my mind finally began to process what I had just read, I looked up at my wife and said "My mother is in the hospital again, and it doesn't look good." She asked me what happened but I had no information to give her at the time. I explained the message from my father and told her we had to wait until later to get answers when my father called.

Later that evening, my father called as promised. I could tell instantly from the sound in his voice that this was indeed serious and he was in pain. He started to tell me that because my mother had been suffering from cirrhosis of the liver, that her other organs had been working over time to compensate for the livers failure. As time went on the stress of the situation was too much for her other organs and they were starting to shut down. He told me that her liver was not functioning in any kind of way now and that her kidneys were starting to fail.

In complete shock and unable to really process what I was hearing, I asked my father what happens next. He paused for a moment to regain his composure and said "What happens next? Well, we're going to lose her." I could feel my heart shattering to dust. I started to shake and developed a quiver in my voice. As best as I could I asked him if we should head down now, but he told us to hold off for awhile until he had more information. I asked him what kind of time frame were we looking at, and he told me they really didn't know at the moment.

Struggling even harder to keep myself together I told my father to keep me up to date and call me any time he learned new information. We said our goodbyes after the short conversation so that he could call my brothers and tell them the sorrowful news. I'm sure those must have been some of the most difficult phone calls he ever had to make. Not only was he on the verge of losing the love of his life, but he now had to tell all his children that they were about to lose their mother.

When I hung up with my father I conveyed all the new information to my wife, listening to myself talk I couldn't believe what I was saying. I didn't think I would have to say things like that about my mother for a long time. We all had expected her to live a long and healthy life. Unfortunately, the truth was we were all about to face the hardest most painful moment in our lives.

Not knowing what was going to happen and when, we started to discuss canceling our vacation and rescheduling it for another time. It was more bad news having to cancel our much needed vacation, but by then I didn't really care. I couldn't think of going anywhere other than to see my mother. Even if she was given a few weeks to live and we still could have gone I would have been miserable and it would have just been a waste.

Come Wednesday I went on with my scheduled chemo treatment while my wife called to rearrange our vacation. To our luck they still had an opening in the next month. Luck, it seems funny to consider that lucky given what was going on at the time. Real luck would be not having this happen at all, but I suppose as I usually say with all the bad things that happen in life there are still good things to be grateful for.

I talked to my father on and off every day getting bits of information as they were passed on to him by the doctors. I told my dad that we had already canceled our vacation and were planning on coming down and again he told us to hold off for awhile, I think mainly he didn't want me to be there day after day just waiting for my mother to die. I know he did it to protect my brothers and me for as long as he could from the whole situation, so there was no way I could be angry with him about telling me not to come.

Finally, on Thursday night while talking with my dad he said that she had taken a turn for the worst and didn't have much time. He said that my brothers Curt and Steve would be headed down on Friday and that I should get there as soon as possible. Since I was in the middle of my chemo treatment I told him that we had already planned to be there on Saturday and that we had begun packing for the trip.

Neither my wife nor I had any clue what to pack for and how long. The best I could do was tell her to be prepared to possibly be there for two weeks since we had no idea how much longer she was going to last and what kind of arrangements were being made for after her death. So in the end we packed for two weeks and brought clothes for a funeral. I didn't want to ask my dad if I should bring clothes for a funeral. He was having a hard enough time at the moment and it just seemed like too painful of a question to ask. The last thing I wanted was to cause more pain for him. So we packed them anyway to be ready.

Friday I went to the doctor's office and had the pump disconnected from my chest. I gassed up the car for the trip and finished packing. By the time the evening rolled around we were ready for our trip, at least travel ready. Mentally and emotionally I was a wreck. Kellee did her best to console me and ease my pain, but no matter what she said or did I felt lost. I knew this day would come at some point but I hadn't expected it so soon nor could I predict just how awful I was going to feel.

With a long ten hour drive ahead of us the next day we went to bed early that night. I had the feeling that I wouldn't be getting much sleep, but I needed as much rest as I could get. Having just come off my last treatment my body was weak and I would need all of my strength to make the long trip. I knew it was going to be hard but I was going to do everything in my power to get to my mother before it was too late. I had to say goodbye her, and be there for her one last time to make it as easy on her as possible.

I can't begin to imaging what goes through someone's mind when they know they are about to die - fears, regrets, sadness...Whatever they may be, I was going to be there for my mother to assure her that she was loved immensely. I know that if I was in her situation the only thing that would make it easier on me would be being surrounded by those that I love, and I was going to do just that.

Chapter 26

An Angel Is Dying Part II

As I had predicted, I didn't sleep much that night. My body was exhausted from the chemotherapy but my mind refused to give me rest. Though I did manage to sleep some, it was not as much as I had needed. The alarm went off in the early hours that Saturday morning and we planned to be out the door no later that 7:00am. We had a ten hour trip by car from Connecticut to Virginia ahead of us and needed to get out the door as early as possible.

While Kellee showered and dressed I started packing the car, by the time she was ready the trunk and back seat were full of everything we could think of packing. The day before, my wife had gone shopping to grab some muffins for us to eat for breakfast. This way we could eat and snack on the go and not have to worry about making and eating a real breakfast. We grabbed the last of our supplies and got in the car. Since I was still tired and weak Kellee took the first shift driving while I did my best to try and get some rest, maybe even some sleep if possible.

With everything set, we said goodbye to our home and headed on our way. We rolled through the hills of northwestern Connecticut and into New York as we made our way towards the highway. Even though there were the usual beautiful sites to see, everything seemed dull and gray to me. The new outlook on life that I had acquired from my near death experience a few months ago seemed to have faded away.

At the moment there seemed to be no good in my life. For the first time in a long time I could not find anything happy to focus on. It felt like all hope had been lost. I have always been the one to say that "No matter what bad things in life may come, there are always good things to be grateful for." It's a frame of mind that I have lived and believed in for a long time. It's what saved my life many years ago when I suffered from depression. I found my way out by changing my outlook on life and have prospered ever since. This time though, the sadness that dwelled in my heart was too much. No wondrous, amazing sites from nature, no kind words from my wife could comfort me and ease the pain in my soul. This time I was going to face the pain head on with no way to escape it.

We drove on through the day making our way down into Pennsylvania. Around noon time we stopped to grab some lunch near the southern border of PA. We talked about trivial subjects as we ate, even though I was hungry I couldn't fully enjoy my lunch because of my symptoms from my last treatment. My stomach was still questionable and I could barely drink my iced tea due to my cold sensitivity, so I picked and sipped while we talked and rested.

Since we were now about half way there I decided to take over behind the wheel and give my wife a break. At least it might help take my mind off everything while I concentrated on driving. We continued on our way through the rest of the states until finally arriving in Virginia later that afternoon.

By around 5:00pm we finally arrived at my parent's house in Bedford. My dad was at the hospital with my mom and had left my brothers Curt and Steve there with my grandmother. When we pulled in the drive way I was greeted by my brother Curt who led us into my grandmother's module home. Inside, Curt's girlfriend and my brother Steve sat talking with my grandmother. All of them greeted me with sorrowful smiles and my grandmother reached out for me to give her a hug.

We sat and talked for a bit while we waited for my dad to return. The plan was for him to come back with some dinner for us to eat, after which we would make the trip to the hospital and spend some time with my mother. About a half hour later my dad returned with some pizzas for us to eat, though he had a smile on his face as usual and was very happy to see my wife and I, I could see the pain in his eyes.

It reminded me of when I was a kid and my parents were considering divorce. In my whole life I had never seen nor heard my dad cry until they separated and considered divorce. To my knowledge, he hadn't cried again since then. Now that he was about to lose his wife forever all those familiar pains were coming back to him and forcing their way to the surface.

Once we had said our hellos, we gathered everyone into the house to eat. For my brothers and father it had been the first real meal they had eaten in days. My dad had been so busy looking after my mom at the hospital that he just never had time to eat. Many people, when in such a horrible situation, don't give much thought to eating.

We made idle chat as we ate, I guess we were all doing our best to make light of the situation and keep each others spirits up. So for most of the conversation we avoided the obvious topic that was on all of our minds. A lot of the time was filled with nothing more than the sound of us all chewing on our much needed sustenance. It was one of those times that you don't realize how hungry you really are until you start to eat.

We downed the pizza in less than a few minutes, gorging ourselves until we felt full enough to move on. Once our hunger had been satisfied, we packed up the rest and put it away in the fridge and began to prepare our selves for the short, yet long, journey to the hospital.

My wife and I went with my brother Stephen and my dad in his car, while my brother Curt and his girlfriend followed in the car they had rented for the weekend. It had been several years since I had been down to my parent's house. Prior to this visit I had only been here once with Kellee and her parents to spend Thanksgiving with my parents. However the last time I was there I was laid out for most of the trip due to an injury to my shoulder. I had caused some serious damage to my shoulder years ago while working for a moving company and once every few years the old injury would spark up and cause me pain and discomfort for a few days. Usually it was very minor and I could still function, but hat time I had lost most of the use of my arm and spent much of the time at my parent's house sitting in a chair loaded up on pain killers. I was glad to be there, but it was a huge disappointment because I never got to see the area my parents lived in. We arrived in the dark and I spent the whole time there in a chair trying to get better while my dad took my wife and her parents on a tour of the area.

Now, finally, I would get my chance to see where my parents lived and what the town was like. It was just very unfortunate that it took these particular circumstances to bring me back down there. I had already been planning on making a trip down to spend Christmas with my parents and really get my fill of the area, but now all those plans had disappeared.

We made our way down some back roads and finally hit the main stretch of town. It was a quaint little quiet town. It reminded me a lot of where I lived, only more farm like. Being that it was in the south it just had a different feel than northern country. The mountains and trees may look the same but there is just an all around different atmosphere there.

Driving through town I recognized some chain stores that I was familiar with and some that I had never seen before. The place felt familiar yet not at the same time, I found myself staring out the window as if I was looking for a place that I knew, yet it was impossible since I had never been here before. I suppose that I was seeking comfort by trying to find something familiar to me - some sort of piece of home to help ease the pain. I found nothing.

We talked and made small jokes on the way to the hospital. Again all of us were doing our best to make light of the situation. The rest of the evening would be spent saying goodbye to the woman we all loved and cherished. At this point the severity of the situation had not fully sunk in to me. Curt and Steve had already seen our mother that morning. My brother Jay had not arrived yet. I had no idea what to expect, no clue as to just how painful the nights events were going to be. Like I had mentioned before, even when you know you're about to lose someone and you think you are prepared, you really aren't. There is no way to prepare for just how painful it truly is. Losing someone is painful enough, but I was about to experience something much worse than just losing my mom.

The ride lasted about a half hour before we arrived at the hospital. Stepping out of the car I started to try to prepare myself mentally and emotionally for what was about to come. We waited a moment for my brother to park and join us as we headed towards the entrance of the hospital. Having been sick myself for the last few months I had had my fill of hospitals and doctor's offices. Walking into them just seemed to give me a feeling of despair, and this time was no different.

We went in the entrance and made our way down the hall towards my mother's room. At this point I was still a blank slate. No one had informed me of her condition, so I really had no idea what to expect when I walked through the door. In my own mind I thought I would see her lying on a bed very quiet, we would walk in, wake her up, and she would smile and say hello and we would get to talk. I could not have been any farther from the truth.

As I entered her room I almost stopped dead in my tracks, there was my mother lying in bed, choking, struggling to breathe and finding no relief. My heart just about gave in at that moment and I almost started crying right away. We all rushed to her side to try and find out what was wrong and why she was having so much trouble breathing. There was a nurse in the room at the time that had just finished changing her sheets and was totally ignoring her as she struggled for air. Had I not been able to keep my composure for my mom I would have been extremely irate with the woman and yelled at her until she herself cried. We quickly discovered that by tilting the bed up she was finally able to clear the fluids from her throat and breathe again. A few moments passed as she tried to catch her breath and she realized that we were all there to see her. Although my brothers and father had been there earlier that day, she had been asleep and totally out of it, not seeming to be aware of their presence. Now though she was awake and aware we were there. With what little strength she had she gave us all a big smile. We each greeted her with hugs and kisses and stood by her bed side comforting her as best as we could.

Prior to this I had not seen my mother in over a year. Her bouts with illness along with my own prevented us both from seeing one another. I stood by her bedside looking down at her with a crushing heart. I hate to say it, but she looked awful. She almost didn't look like herself. Her hair was almost all gray and brittle looking, her skin color was an awful pale shade somewhere between gray and yellow, and because of the fluids building up in her she was swollen from head to toe. She was struggling to breathe, taking in a deep breath every few seconds. Because she was so weak and had fluid building up in her body she could not breathe normally anymore - just a deep breath every few moments as she clung to life for as long as she could.

I think it was at that moment seeing how frail she looked that it really set in that she was in fact going to die. Inside I was crying like a lost child, abandoned without hope, with out love, only knowing fear and heart ache. On the outside I did my best to keep my composure, I choked down all the tears and kept them from surfacing. I knew if I let them out I would not be able to control myself and wouldn't be able to stop. It wasn't that I was trying to be a strong, tough man, I guess in my mind I didn't want her to see me cry. I didn't want her to see me in pain, I just wanted to be there to comfort her and keep her as positive as possible.

I gently caressed her forehead with my hand, brushing her hair away from her face, making as much physical contact as possible to let her know I was there. My brothers each held one of her hands and did the same. Curt's girlfriend stood by his side doing her best to comfort him. She held him from his side and gently ran her hand up and down his arm. I'm sure her gentle touch and her support helped him a lot.

My wife stood somewhat in the background giving me time with my mother, every now and then I would go to her for a hug. This was the most difficult thing I had ever been through in my life and I was glad to have her there. Had she not been there I am certain I would have lost control of all of my emotions.

My father stood at the foot of his wife's bed, looking at her with a longing only a husband and wife could understand when you're about to lose one another forever. He took the time to explain to us all what was happening with her and why she looked the way she did. It pained him to talk about it and he had to periodically excuse him self to go into the bathroom to gather himself together. I could hear the pain and sorrow in his voice each time he started to break down as he would head to the bathroom for a tissue. Here was my father who had always been a strong figure my whole life, now at his weakest. I had never seen him so vulnerable before. The only thing I could do was embrace him and try my best to console him.

My mother in such a weakened state that she slipped in and out of consciousness often. Each time she would fall asleep we would back off for awhile to let her rest and talk and console each other. My brother Steve looked very lost. His wife could not make the trip since she had their two sons to look after and could not get away from work. I could tell he felt alone. Looking at him and seeing the pain in his eyes I asked if he needed a hug too. At the moment I was half heartedly joking, but it was an open invitation. He paused for a moment then latched on to me, I held on to him and did what I could to let him know that he wasn't alone. We were all there for each other.

At one point while she slept we were talking about a store back in Pennsylvania that was a favorite of both my mom and my wife. We were talking about how Curt's girlfriend had never been there and joking about how when Curt finally took her she would never want to leave. Not realizing that my mother was now awake I joked about how we shouldn't mention the store because my mother might here it and hop out of bed and push us all out of the way and jump in the car to do some shopping. We realized she was awake when a huge smile came across her face. We all noticed it at the same time and for the first time that day felt a sense of calmness in seeing her beautiful smile once more.

For the first time since hearing that we were going to lose her, my heart filled with joy at the site of seeing happiness on her face. I smiled back at her and quickly walked to the side of her bed to hug her. I held her gently for a moment, not wanting to squeeze her and apply any pressure to her already painfully stretched skin.

We stayed there a few hours going back and forth between comforting my mom and each other. As the night drew closer my mother appeared to be experiencing more and more pain. She clenched onto her sheets and constantly squirmed about, and would occasionally squeeze her eyes shut when the pain became too much. Seeing how much pain she was in we called a nurse to come in and give her something for the pain so she wouldn't suffer during her last hours. The nurse obliged and used a small syringe to squirt a liquid pain killer into her mouth. After a few moments she began to settle and soon fell asleep.

We all stood and watched over her for awhile, now that she was asleep it was the first time since we had arrived that we saw her calm and without pain. She continued to only take a breath every few seconds, and at times scared us when there would be a long pause between each breath making us think she had passed. We would all stop and hold our own breath to see if she had indeed left us, but each time she would eventually take in a deep breath and give us all a sigh of relief when we knew she was still with us.

Realizing that there was nothing more we could do that evening and since it had been a very long day for my wife and me, we all decided to head on home and wait for the morning when we would return. The drive back to my parent's home was much quieter than the drive to the hospital. All of us were in a great deal of pain and struggled to keep our emotions together. We talked here and there but for the most part the drive was silent.

I wasn't sure if I was going to get much sleep that night. I was exhausted from the long drive and the after effects of my last chemo treatment, but with the thoughts of my mother on my mind I felt like it might be yet another restless night. Kellee and I made our bed and got into our pajamas. We said goodnight to my father and brothers and crawled into bed. I'm not a particularly religious person, but before I went to sleep I prayed for my mother, I asked that she be looked after and that her pain and suffering would be no more. With that thought in my mind I closed my eyes and went to sleep.

Chapter 27

Death Of An Angel

That night I managed to get some real sleep. Although I woke constantly to change positions, I managed to sleep more than I thought I would. I was exhausted both physically and emotionally. The stress of the situation had worn me out, and for the first time in days I finally was able to get some sleep.

That night, or rather early in the morning just before sunrise, I had a very vivid dream. I have never been one to preach my beliefs to people. Some people believe in religion, others don't. Some believe in things like ghosts and psychic abilities, and others think it's just plain foolish. That night however I had a dream about my mother that left me with more questions than answers. In my dream I was entering her hospital room and she was lying in her bed. She sat up with a smile and got out of bed and gave me a big long hug. I told her that I loved her and would miss her and she just smiled back at me and told me she loved me too. Then as I stood looking at her she said goodbye and disappeared.

Just as quick as the dream had started it was over and I shot awake. Moments later I heard my father walking around upstairs waking my bothers and when he came down to the living room where Kellee and I were sleeping he said he had gotten a phone call from the hospital and we need to head down there. I asked him what was going on and he looked at me with tears in his eyes and with a crackled voice he said that we had lost her. My eyes welled up and I walked over and held on tight to him as we both cried.

After we calmed ourselves down I let him continue on to get ready to go to the hospital. I sat down for a moment thinking about what had just happened and my dream. As I said I never preach my beliefs to anyone so my dream is open to interpretation. Some will think of it as just a dream, just my subconscious mind projecting my thoughts from the previous day into a cinema for my mind. For me it seemed as real as life and was in a sense a comforting thought that I was able to say goodbye to my mother, whether it was real or just a dream it meant something to me.

Regaining my composure, I hurried around gathering my clothes to get dressed. Slowly but surely my brothers did the same and soon down stairs to join us. Having received such horrible news none of us really had much to say to one another. In a daze we all did what we needed to do in order to get ready to go to the hospital.

Kellee and I again got into the car with my father and my brother Steve, while Curt and his girlfriend followed us in their car like before. This car ride was a lot quieter than the one from the previous night. I'm sure all of us were lost in thought and doing what we could to keep from losing control of our emotions. The ride down seemed to last forever. In a sense I found comfort in that. The longer it took to get to the hospital, the longer it would be before I saw the lifeless vessel that was once my mother.

I don't remember what time it was when we arrived at the hospital, but it didn't matter. Time didn't seem to even exist that day. After we parked we all took a deep breath and made our way into the hospital. We walked passed the front desk and continued down the hall to my mother's room, with a pause we opened the door and slowly entered the room. Once again I was completely unprepared for what I was about to see, and I know I wasn't the only one. It was the most heartbreaking site I had ever seen in my entire life. Any and all joy that I had ever had inside of me died that moment, some of which has never returned, and probably never will.

There in the bed lay my mother lifeless. She drew no breath. She didn't stir when we entered the room. She lied there still and quiet, her mouth open as if she had struggled to take her last breath. She was gone. I would never hear her voice again, never make her smile again, never hear her tell me that she loves me. All of that was gone forever except for in my memories which I hold dear and will do so forever.

My father and my brothers gathered around her, kissing her on the forehead and gently caressing her face as they said goodbye to her. I never made it to my mother's bedside. I stood a few feet away holding my wife and watched them as they said their goodbyes to her. I don't really know why I stood so far away. I guess part of me knew that I wouldn't be able to handle touching her lifeless body, and part of me knew that what was in that bed wasn't my mother anymore. She was gone. The spark that was her essence had left her body and moved on.

At one point my father left the room to call the funeral home to make arrangements for her body to be picked up and moved to their location for one final goodbye before she was cremated. When my father returned he struggled to talk as he told us what the preparations were. He had brought with him a dress that my mother bought in Hawaii that she loved dearly and had asked them to dress her in it for her final viewing later that day.

We soon left the hospital to head home and wait for the call from the funeral home. My grandmother and my mother's sister would also be going for the final viewing. The ride back to my parent's house was difficult, all of us had lost someone who meant the world to us and we all struggled with our emotions in our own way.

Eventually we made it home. Like before the car ride seemed to last forever, with nothing but painful thoughts and memories. Time seemed to stretch on indefinitely. Once we had arrived, my father went over to see my grandmother and my mother's sister to inform them of the plans. The rest of us gathered on the front deck and made small talk to try to pass time. We talked about childhood memories, places we had gone, things we had done. We did our best to talk about happy things to help drown out the pain we were all experiencing.

Later in the day we received the phone call from the funeral home. All of the preparations had been made and it was time to say one final

The Crappiest Year Ever

farewell. Once again, we all packed ourselves into the cars and headed back into town. We arrived at the funeral home and all of us took turns helping our grandmother through the parking lot and inside. She had been struggling the last few years with walking, so with the help of her walker and all of us we eventually made it inside.

We slowly walked through the den and into the viewing room. There in her dress from Hawaii lay my mother. Motionless, not one breath did she take, all life gone from her. Slowly everyone gathered around her to say goodbye and once again I found myself unable to get within a few feet of her. Just like before I clung on to my wife for support and watched everyone else say goodbye. I was frozen in place, but it wasn't from fear. Like before, the last thing I wanted to do was touch the cold lifeless body of what was once my mother. Of all the painful memories that were already stuck in my head, that is one which I could never bear to have in my mind the rest of my life.

As my family said their goodbyes, I stood silent just holding on to my wife, painful thoughts flashed into my mind one after another. She was gone forever leaving me with many happy memories from a life filled of love, but also the unrelenting painful memories of her last few hours in this world that would haunt me forever. This was the hardest, most painful experience in my life that I had ever gone through. I could never imagine that it would be as difficult to deal with as it was. I again owe my wife more than I can ever express in words. Her being by my side was the only thing that kept me together through the whole event.

As a child you never think about losing your parents. In a child's mind time seems to stretch on forever. Summers last a life time and each year seems like a millennium. So to a child your parents have lived forever already and will be around until the end of time. As we grow older and learn more about the world we finally realize not just our own mortality, but we also learn that one day those who brought us into this world will cease to exist.

We all pray and hope that it's something that we will not have to deal with for a long time. We expect our mothers and fathers to live a long time like their parents and have a chance to enjoy their golden years. So when you do lose your mother or father so early in life, I would imagine it to be more painful than if they had been able to live a long and full life, not one that was cut so short. I say this because it leaves you thinking about what little time you did have with them, and the time and experiences you lost out on that would have come in the next few decades.

Granted, my mother lived long enough to see her children grow up, and even meet some of her grandchildren. Her life was still short. If she had not become ill, she easily could have lived for another thirty years or so and had the opportunity to spend more time with those she loved. Being twenty-nine when she died, I myself still felt as if I were still a child who expected to still have my mother in my life for a long time until I was old and gray, but that dream has been taken from me.

Chapter 28

Ease His Pain

Later in the day after we returned from the funeral home, my brothers began to pack their stuff and get ready to head home. They wanted to stay, but unfortunately my brother Curt could not get any more time off from work so they were forced to head home. Once they had finished packing the car, they said their goodbyes to us and headed back home to Pennsylvania.

Earlier in the day my wife and I decided that since it was just going to be us and my father we would take him out to dinner. He had not eaten a real meal in days, and in all honesty we all needed to go somewhere to put our minds off things for awhile. So as mid-afternoon approached we decided where to go, and as a special treat I gave my father the keys to my new BMW and told him he could drive. Until this visit he hadn't seen the car in person and was thrilled to not only see it, but have a chance to drive it.

We piled into the car and headed off. Driving my car put a much needed smile on my fathers face. I watched him as he drove and could see he was really enjoying himself on the roads as he dove into the corners. Weaving back and forth on the wavy country roads took his mind off things and for the first time I'm sure in a long time, he was enjoying himself.

The rest of the evening was spent eating, drinking, and enjoying one another's company. We told old stories and new ones, we shared the story of our trip down, and the places we had been in the past few years since the last time we saw him. It was nice to spend some time alone with my dad and to bring a smile to his face. We each fed off of each other's sympathy and had a relaxing fun evening.

When we had finished dinner I again handed my dad the keys to my car and told him to have some fun and drive us home. With out hesitation he took the keys from my hand and off we went. Like before a smile came to his face as he drove and I explained all technical highlights of the car which brought about more excitement in him. Seeing how happy he was and how much fun he was having put all of us in a better mood. We soon arrived back and my parents home and spent the rest of the evening recouping from the day and watching TV.

The next day my father took us on a scenic tour of the area. We went on the Blue Ridge Parkway which zigzagged up and down the Blue Ridge Mountains. We stopped at all the scenic over-looks we could to take photos and admire the views. It was a comforting change of pace to do something we enjoyed. My father took us to all of the best spots with the most breathtaking views and told us about some of the area's history.

Most of the day was spent just driving around and getting to see a lot of the area we had never been to before. We stopped at one point for lunch to "recharge our batteries" as we like to say in my family. My father took us to a bagel shop and told us a funny story about the place. When I was young, my family lived on Long Island New York and my father worked in New York City. Sure enough we had bagels from time to time, and a lot of people will agree that New York makes some of the best bagels in the world.

Well my father had discovered the place while driving around one day and decided to stop in and grab a bite to eat. He ordered his food, sat and ate it, and when he was finished he called over the owner. He told her that it was the best bagel he had eaten since he worked and lived in New York, which was well over ten years ago. The woman smiled and said thank you and then told my father that they were in fact New York bagels. They are made and delivered straight from New York to her store every few days.

When we finished with lunch we continued our tour. We went to visit some lake resort that was quite a drive away, and then made our way back towards my father's home to rest for awhile before we went out for dinner again. Kellee and I had decided that since my brother Jayson was going to be flying in late that night that we would head back the next day. Then Jayson would be with my father for a few days to make sure he was okay. Since it was our last night together, my father decided to treat us to dinner as a way of saying thank you for all we had done. Just like the night before we spent the evening relaxing, eating, enjoying a few drinks, and taking comfort in each other's company.

Since my brother was going to be flying in fairly late, Kellee and I decided to turn in early and try to get as much sleep as possible for the ten hour drive we had to make the next day. The following morning we packed up the car and woke my brother to say hello and goodbye. He was disappointed that we had to leave so soon, and we wished we could stay, but work duties were calling us back home. Once we were certain my father was taken care of, we headed home.

Chapter 29

The Truth

The first few days home were extremely rough on my wife and me. I was still very torn up about losing my mother to the point where I started to shut her out. It wasn't that I didn't want to talk about it, I just wasn't ready. It was too painful to even speak about. Every time I closed my eyes I could see images as clearly as day of my mother lying in that hospital bed suffering. Every night as I lay in bed trying to fall asleep it was all I could think about and all I could picture in my head. It was eating me alive.

Meanwhile, I had no idea what my wife was going through. I knew she wanted to talk, but I thought it was just for me. I thought she wanted to console me, but as it turned out she was suffering as well. She had disturbing images of my mother stuck in her mind that were eating away at her day and night. Had I known this at the time, I would have made the effort to talk to her about it no matter how painful it might have been for me.

One evening before bed it all finally exploded, she couldn't hold it in any longer and I quickly learned just how hard the whole experience had been on my wife. For the first time since we had left Virginia I was being confronted face to face with all the painful memories that had been building up inside me. Seeing how much suffering my wife had been going through all this time made the situation even worse. I hated seeing her in pain. It killed me. I had no strength left in me now and I finally broke down into tears.

We lay in bed for a few hours talking and holding one another as we finally got everything out in the open. We took turns consoling one another as we talked, she told me of her nightmares, her fears, and the images that haunted her non-stop. I could feel my heart breaking again, crying out In agony for some kind of relief. It hadn't been long since my mothers passing, so all the feelings and thoughts were still fresh in my mind. It was hard to talk about everything because of this, but over the course of a few hours we managed to pry out the painful memories that had been haunting us both.

We hadn't realized it, but it had gotten pretty late. We had been talking for hours trying to make one another feel better. At one point I noticed the clock and how late it was and since both of us had to be up early for work the next morning we called it quits for the night. By now we were both drained physically and emotionally. With an uncomfortable silence we both finished getting ready for bed. We climbed under the sheets and each laid there staring up at the ceiling. After awhile she fell asleep and I continued to struggle to rid my mind of the images of my mother. I hardly slept that night, all the things we talked about kept rolling through my mind.

I tossed and turned all night long, and when I did sleep I had nightmares about my mother. Before I knew it morning had come and it was time to get up for work. Exhausted, I struggled to make it through the day which seemed to drag on for an eternity. This cycle repeated it self day after day, night after night. Every night I lay in bed, haunted by painful images. I barely got any sleep anymore, and so every day I was completely drained.

Chapter 30

Support

Come Monday morning with still hardly any sleep, I dragged myself out of bed and headed off to the doctor's office for my next chemotherapy treatment. Once again I sat in the chair, looking around the room at the other suffering lost souls. With each visit I had to not only physically prep myself but mentally as well. At times it can be a pretty traumatic experience being surrounded by other people fighting for their lives, being stuck in the chest over and over again with needles, and having poison force fed into your body. It's not an easy thing for anyone to go through. It's made even worse as the next few days roll by and the side effects start to come about.

Each time I received my treatment and had the pump hooked up to me for forty six straight hours, I was confined to my couch in my living room. I found myself drained of all energy, sick to my stomach, and running to the bathroom constantly as my body tried to flush out the poison running through my veins. I tried to stay strong and positive with each treatment, but sometimes it was just too much to handle and I would feel depressed for several days. It was made even worse knowing that I would have to do this over and over again for several months.

Just like with any kind of illness or depressing situation, some can handle it better than others. A lot of people were fairly surprised at how well I took everything when I learned of my condition and how I handled suffering every other week for days at a time. As hard as it was for the most part I did remain positive, I knew it would be over soon and that I would beat cancer. I had come this far, and I would be damned if I would just give up and lose faith.

Not everyone has my strength though. I particularly remember one visit to the doctor's office that I will never forget. I was in my usual chair receiving my in-office treatment when a new face arrived. She sat in the chair next to mine, separated only by a small cabinet. At first I didn't pay much attention to her. I had been there a few times by now and it was common to see new faces. Mid-way through this woman's chemo treatment she began to rock back and forth. Before I knew it, she was crying and talking to herself. For the first time since I had been diagnosed with cancer, I saw just how much it affects some people and pulls apart their lives.

To this day I still don't know what exactly she was crying about. It could have been that in her mind getting cancer was a definite death sentence. Or perhaps the whole experience of receiving chemo and its side-effects were too much for her. For me the whole experience had been fairly easy, but it was then that I realized just how much it affects people differently.

I have received so much bad news in my life over the years that now it barely ever fazed me anymore. I had grown strong because of it and know that I can beat or survive just about anything that is thrown my way, and I take great pride in that. As strong as I am I can't take full credit for my strength. A lot of it comes from the support of my family and friends.

Being a huge car nut, I am part of a large online community of other people who are just as passionate about cars as I am. In particular the community I am most active in is a BMW fan site called Bimmer Forums or BFC for short. Most of the site is dedicated to our passion for BMWs, helping one another keep our cars on the road, and sharing our progress as we build project cars.

However, there is a small section on the site dedicated to everything else in the world where we gather and talk about anything and everything that isn't about cars. Over the years I have made a few friends that despite having never met them in person, I consider them to be good friends that I could trust.

When I found out about my condition, I made an announcement on the site that I had been diagnosed with cancer and was about to begin a battle for my life. I'm not totally certain why I decided to tell complete strangers about something so personal. I guess part of me just wanted to get it out whether or not anyone even cared or noticed. To my surprise, the few friends I had made over the years each reached out to me privately and offered me support for my up-coming battle.

The first was my friend, Jack, also known as Sneezy on the forum. He informed me that he himself once had a battle with cancer and knew exactly what I was going through. He offered me an ear to listen if I ever needed to vent my frustrations. After him, my other friends Jen, Sachin, and Rob (aka Sparkchaser – the hipster) all reached out to me. Sachin even went as far as to send me a book about his personal hero and his trials of life that he himself overcame. Last, but not least, there is also M Shareef whose kind words and thoughts helped spark the idea of putting my story into words and creating this book.

Their support gave me strength to push on and never give up. As time went on, other people that I never knew joined in and offered me support and comfort. Some even offered gifts to cheer me up or money to help pay bills. I turned down all the offerings, but in turn only asked for their support. That was all I ever needed or wanted from anyone.

To most people the whole situation might seem odd, but not to us. We are a tight knit community that for the most part looks out for one another. Any time any one of us has had to deal with a difficult situation in life everyone bands together and offers help and support. Sure we don't all always see eye to eye, but when someone is in need all discrepancies are put aside in favor of offering a lending hand.

With each passing treatment I was encouraged by the members to keep fighting, constantly being told that I would beat it and that their thoughts and prayers were with me. It was then that I really started to realize that I wasn't going through this alone, I had people that I didn't even know wishing me a speedy recovery. In a world where it seems that no one cares about anyone but themselves, it was nice to see that in spite of all the horrible people that exist in the world, there are still those who would put others before themselves and offer a complete stranger a helping hand. It gives me a small bit of hope to know that not all of humanity has been lost in man, perhaps some day the world will change for the better once they realize we need to help one another in order to survive.

Chapter 31

Never Alone

As the next few weeks went by, I continued to struggle with the death of my mother while at the same time dealing with my battle against cancer. It was a lot for any one person to endure, and I would never look down on someone that could not handle being in a situation like I was. It was the most difficult time in my life, and had I not had the support that I did from my family and friends, I would have lost all faith in myself and in life.

Each day was a trial on my strength and my will to continue on. Every night I still found myself spending several hours trying to get to sleep, only to be confronted with painful visions in my head of my mother suffering. Most nights it became too much to bear and I would break down crying. It wasn't just the fact that I had lost my mother, but that she suffered during her last days on earth. Seeing her in as much pain as she was in, was just as heartbreaking, if not more, than the fact that she was dying. No one deserves to suffer like that in the end.

Every night I was haunted by those memories, I was suffering tremendously inside, and for reasons that I don't even know, I chose to face them alone. I'm sure if I would have woken up my wife she would have consoled me, but every night I did my best to be as quiet as possible as I wiped away the tears from my face. Thinking back to how difficult it was for me, I can only imagine how hard it must have been for my father. Worrying about him, I checked up on him frequently to show that I cared and assure him that he wasn't alone.

People often give me credit for being such a strong person for having endured so much in such a short period of time. The truth is that as strong as I may seem to be, I wouldn't be this way with out my friends and family. Knowing how much they cared and how hard they tried to keep me positive, helped me more than they will ever know. I also drew great strength from what to me was a very unlikely source. As I mentioned earlier complete strangers were more than willing to do anything in their power that they could to help me.

For anyone out there that feels alone, you're not. You're never truly alone. You aren't the only one suffering. You aren't the only one in the world who is fighting for your life. If you feel brave enough, reach out to someone and tell them your story. Never be afraid to ask for help. As I have come to learn, there are plenty of people who are more than willing to listen and offer you help in any way they can, even if it's just a listening ear. Often that is all some people need - just someone to talk to, a sympathetic ear.

Most of my life, I was the person who would never ask for help. This was not because I was proud, but because I was afraid. I was afraid of being rejected, afraid that no one cared enough about me to really help me. I had always felt alone from as long back as I can remember simply because I was afraid of everyone. I was worried that what I thought about myself was what others thought about me and that it might just be true if I ventured to find out. I know now that I was wrong. I could not have been more wrong. As hard as that was to go through the years alone, I also benefited from that experience. The years I spent isolating myself taught me to be independent. I'm stronger now because of it, but no one is strong enough to not need help from time to time.

In a world where everyone feels like they are alone, the truth is you're not. I spent my whole life believing that, and now I know better. I know that not everyone is a jerk who wants nothing more than to make others suffer. Despite all of the cruel people out there in the world who feel so insecure about themselves that they make others lives miserable, there are still good people out there that you can depend on. The world is a scary place, and for many years it frightened me, but I know now that I won't ever have to face it alone.

Chapter 32

Heaven

It was now mid August, summer's end was closing in and soon the leaves would be changing and the warm welcoming temperatures would begin to give way to cold chilly mornings and dawn's glistening frost. The days were slowly getting shorter hinting at falls arrival, but it was still pleasant enough for Kellee and I to enjoy our vacation at last. It was a month behind schedule, but finally we could take our vacation.

Just like before, the weeks leading up to it we made our plans and began to make arrangements for our absence from work. Luckily, this time around I had several days to recuperate from my last chemotherapy treatment before making the trip. This meant that my side effects would be at their least and that my wife and I would be able to fully enjoy our time away.

Feeling like a blessing had been brought upon us, we were very confident that this would be a great vacation. We knew that for the few days we were gone we would be able forget all of our troubles and escape into a world of care-free thoughts where nothing mattered. When the day finally came, we packed up the car and with smiles on both of our faces, we headed north to Maine.

It's about a three to four hour drive depending on traffic but that didn't matter at all. We had made the trip so many times before that by now time passed by so quickly and before we knew it we were there. Even if the drive took longer than normal we didn't care. We were escaping life, escaping our problems, and headed to the place that makes us the happiest.

The drive to Maine passed by in what seemed like a flash, before we knew it we had passed over the border and were closer than ever to ultimate relaxation. We finally exited the highway and made our way through the local roads to our destination.

As we approach our destination, the road leads closer and closer to the shore and without notice you take one final bend in the road and suddenly the ocean appears next to you stretching far and wide. The moment we round that final curve we always put all the windows down in the car and take in deep breaths. We suck in as much of the fresh salt air as we can. We both let out a pleasing sigh as we exhale and comment on how good the air smells. That moment of taking in our first breath of the salted air seems to wash away all our cares and with it all our problems exit our lives as we exhale. It's an intoxicating aroma that not only calms us both, but brings with it, a flood of past years' pleasant memories.

The road curves and sways along the shoreline. With smiles on our faces, we navigate along side the ocean as we come even closer to our final destination. As we pass through the town our eyes start dancing back and forth between the shops, people, and the ocean, it's an overflow of excitement for the senses.

We have a tradition that after we arrive at the hotel, we park the car and walk back into town to grab some lunch at one of our favorite places. Kellee and I always get the same meal year after year and wash it all down with a bowel of the best ice cream. It's our first official act of being on vacation, and from then on it just continues to get better. We walk up and down the streets, visiting all the shops and working off the meal we just ate. We spend a few moments in each shop looking for items that we will want to check out later in our time there.

Once we have visited all the stores, we head back to the hotel to check in and make our way to our room. After we have settled in, we take a walk across the street and spend some time walking on the beach. With each step we can both feel the stress of our lives melting away. Since this had been such a horrible year, it was a sensation that had never been more welcomed.

Each morning we rose, went to breakfast, and dressed for the beach. We would spend as much of the day as possible just lying on the beach listening to the sounds of the waves crashing and the seagulls cawing. Doing as little as possible was our only goal. All we wanted to do was relax and enjoy the chance to have nothing to worry about.

Each day that passed was comfortingly always the same. We woke, went to the beach, ate some dinner, and spent the evening strolling on the beach looking for seashells by the light of the moon. I know when most people think of spending a vacation at the beach they automatically head south for warm waters and the last place they would think to go is up north to cold Maine. Yes, the water is colder up there, but it's a refreshing cold. You spend hours baking in the hot sun, then so little as standing knee deep in the water is enough to cool you down instantly. It also happens to be the clearest ocean water I have ever seen which makes it even more inviting.

This year for me spending time in the water wasn't as enjoyable as it was in the past years. My sensitivity to the cold was still with me, so I never ventured more than waist-deep. By then the symptoms were minimal and only brought about a mild discomfort at first. By ignoring the mild pain for awhile it would soon pass and I could fully enjoy the water.

As far as we were concerned, we were in heaven. Nothing could bother us. Each day was spent doing what we wanted to do without a care in the world. For the first time since my life had fallen apart, I was at peace. Nothing was stressing me out and I could feel every inch of my body loosening up. I felt great, I felt alive once again, I had energy, I was happy, and I had finally gotten the escape from my life that I had desperately needed.

Even though we spent an extra day in Maine, it was still too short. Before we knew it, it was time to pack up and head home and bid farewell to our beloved slice of heaven. Depressing as it was to leave, we both, for the first time in a long time, felt good about life. The drive home was fairly quiet as we were both still relaxed from our escape. With the afternoon giving way to evening we arrived back home, unpacked the car, and collapsed into the couch in our living room.

Vacation was now over, tomorrow would bring with it all the stresses we had just washed away, but at least now we would be starting with a fresh slate and it would be a little easier to cope with. The sun soon set and it was time for us to climb into bed and dream away the night with thoughts of our beloved Maine.

Chapter 33

Struggling

The weeks seemed to be passing by more quickly than before with each week bringing us closer to the end of my treatments. Although they seemed to be going faster, the end still seemed to be far away, almost like an unattainable dream. It's just one of those situations where the more you want something, the longer it takes to get and it just makes you want it more.

By now my symptoms from the chemotherapy were lasting much longer than they had before. I wasn't recuperating as fast as I used to and some of the more annoying side effects were beginning to linger. Most notably was the numbness in my finger tips and on the bottom of my feet. My sense of touch in both extremities was very dull. It felt as if I had laid on my arm or leg in a funny position and pinched a nerve which caused a pins-and-needles sensation, only this time it wouldn't go away. My doctor told me it would get worse before it would get better and that after my final treatment, it could take weeks or even a few months before the nerves would return to normal.

This only added to the frustration I was experiencing. Not only did I have to subject myself to being poisoned every other week, but now I wasn't able to feel anything with my hands or even feel the ground I walked on. It might be hard to understand just how it can be to lose feeling in your hands. To some it might not seem like such a big deal, but once you have experienced it and realize just how hard it can make some of the smallest tasks, it quickly becomes clear just how much we take little things for granted.

Holding small objects like screws became one of the most difficult, frustrating situations I encountered. Working on some small projects while stuck at home became large chores. Simple tasks that normally would only take a few minutes were now taking me a half hour or more.

With no sense of touch I was constantly dropping things, putting them in wrong or fumbling with them continuously.

I'm normally a very patient person but not being able to do the simple things I enjoyed was making me very bitter. Unfortunately for my friends and family I was starting to develop a short fuse and blow up over just about anything. The stress of it all was starting to turn me into a jerk. I no longer had patience for anything. Once I had realized what was happening I had to constantly monitor myself. I was the one suffering. There was no reason for me to take it out on anyone else. It wasn't their fault.

Thinking back to the whole situation, I guess it's easy to say that I was angry with what had happened to me. It just didn't seem fair that I had to go through this, I had dealt with a lot of crap in my life and now as a kicker life hands me cancer and takes away two dearly loved family members. Then slowly but surely, tasks become more difficult and I didn't have the energy or the patience I used to have. It's a lot for anyone to deal with and try to control.

There were some days when even if nothing had gone wrong, I was just in an extremely foul mood. I was mad that I had to deal with this. It wasn't fair. Why me? Why do these things always happen to me? I started to look back on my life and question the choices I had made. If fate really does exist, what did I do that was so bad that I had to be punished in this way? If there is a god, why does he hate me so much that I am forever cursed to deal with this illness?

All of those questions would just rattle around in my brain constantly to the point of almost driving me mad. I couldn't grasp the idea of why this had to happen to me. I knew then as I do now that there was no one to blame, it was just the cards I were dealt, but I still couldn't help but feel cursed. All I ever wanted was a nice simple happy life with my wife. I gave up on dreams of being big and powerful. None of that was important to me anymore. All that I wanted, all that mattered was that I was with my wife and we were happy.

Now however the happiness was gone. Although the outlook was positive that I would win this battle, and I refused to give up, the fear of me dying would always be in the back of my wife's and my minds. We would never be free of this curse. It would be with us forever. As a result of all this I was starting to succumb to depression again. It was getting harder to push out the negative thoughts and keep myself positive. I started looking to my friends and family more for support. For their own good I still put on a brave face, but I am sure some were able to see past it and understand that I was afraid, and at times, losing hope.

I knew then, just as I know now that I wasn't being singled out in life, there are plenty of others who suffer from this disease or something worse. I was fortunate to be alive and still have those around who cared about me. Yet I still started to fall into the helpless trap of depression so many others do. It was going to be a long hard journey to pull myself back out of it, but thankfully I wasn't going to do it alone.

Chapter 34

Storms On The Horizon

Summer was coming to an end which here on the east puts us right in middle of hurricane season. Normally this isn't such a big deal to those who live in the Northeast, but this year things would be different. Once every few years, the stars align just perfectly and one major storm will work its way up north. A tropical storm had started to develop just off of the coast of Florida which would soon come to be known as Hurricane Irene. All the weather maps and forecasts predicted her path would take her right up the east coast and slam right into Connecticut. Sure enough, as it gained strength and climbed its way north, it set its eye on us and never looked back.

The week that the hurricane was scheduled to hit also happened to be a week when I would be doing one of my treatments. So, naturally my wife and I stayed glued to the weather reports every day to see just what we could be expecting. To our relief, as the storm climbed north it began to lose strength. As it drew closer to Connecticut, it lost its hurricane status and was dropped back down to a tropical storm, which while still dangerous, was not as powerful or ominous as a hurricane.

Tropical Storm Irene made land fall in Connecticut on the Sunday before my next treatment, and to our surprise all we had seen through out the day was just rain. Buckets and buckets of rain but hardly any wind, it was calm outside throughout the whole day. Still we continued to check for updates on the storm hoping and praying it would pass us with out trouble.

Later in the evening, the rain started to die down and the clouds started to lighten up, but the wind started to blow a little harder. As the storm began to leave us it was saying farewell with a vengeance. Huge wind gusts swept over the area, trees swayed back and forth looking as though they might snap in half at any moment. Wind gust after wind gust slammed into us causing the power to flicker on and off.

The house in which we live is an old Victorian style home that has been converted into apartments. Old yet strong, the house groaned and creaked in protest from the punishing winds. We had been fortunate that the previous fall the roof, which had been in dire need of replacing for some time, was stripped and refinished. Had it not been done it surely would have been ripped off from the winds or leaked badly from the rain. Thanking our lucky stars that we had a new strong roof over our heads, we hoped for the best.

The power had been struggling to stay on through the barrage of high wind gusts, but at last it was too much. With a long dimming flicker the power faded and disappeared into the dark gloom of the late afternoon sky. Sitting on our couch for awhile Kellee and I waited to see if it would once again return, but as the winds finally died down we came to the realization that we would be spending the rest of the night in complete darkness. Armed with lighters, we walked around the apartment and lit candles. With nothing more we could really do, we broke out the board games and settled in for a few rounds of Scrabble.

Not knowing when the power might return, we began to wonder about my treatment that was scheduled for the next day. If we had lost power there was a good chance that in the next town over where the doctor's office was, they had lost it as well. Knowing that hurricanes can cause massive damage and delay the return of power for a long time, it became apparent that my treatments might be delayed if not for several days, a week or two.

With my appointment scheduled for first thing Monday morning, we decided that we would take our chances and head out to the doctor anyway. When morning arrived we woke and took turns showering by candlelight. Cell phones in hand, we jumped in the car and headed out. As we drove along we took notice of the homes along the road to see if anyone had power. Reaching the outskirts of our town, not one single home showed any signs of light or power of any sort. We continued on our way, avoiding the small fallen branches in the road, watching every house we passed.

It takes about a half hour to get from our home to the doctor's office, and at about twenty minutes in as we approached the town line my phone rang. It was the doctor's office, at first my heart sank thinking they were calling to cancel after we had come all this way. Eager to know, I answered the phone. With a big sigh of relief it was the office calling to make sure we were still coming to our appointment. They had been lucky and never lost power which meant everything would go as planned.

The treatment went on as normal at the office. Meanwhile, we talked with the doctor and nurses and shared our experiences with the storm. Some had lost power like us; others were fortunate and had nothing more than just rain and minor flooding. As the in-office treatment came to an end, Kellee and I started talking about how to prepare for not having power while I continued my treatment at home.

Having never been through anything like this before we weren't really sure how to handle the situation, with no power and me hooked up to medical equipment it was going to be something new. The pump itself runs on batteries so power wasn't an issue for that, but when it came to cooking and spending the next 46 hours stranded on my couch it was going to make this a very miserable time.

With the pump hooked up we were ready to go, my wife and I said our goodbyes and headed home, worrying about the next few days. It's miserable enough when the power goes out, but having to deal with the awful side effects from the chemo drugs on top of it was going to make this power outage even worse.

On the way home we decided we would just take things one step at a time and deal with the problems if any, as they came. After a quiet drive we arrived home and walked up the stairs to our apartment. With a turn of the knob we entered our home to be greeted by the sound of our fridge humming away with power as it pumped out cold air to cool our food once more.

Huge smiles began to grow on both of our faces. All the fears which built up on the drive home had instantly washed away as we stepped into our apartment and discovered that we once again had power. We had caught a huge break this time, finally something had gone our way and this treatment would be no worse than the others.

Though we lucked out this time, come the end of October when I would be doing my final chemo treatment, lady luck once again looked the other way and turned her back on us. Another storm was brewing; a classic "nor'easter" as they call it was headed our way and was bringing with it an unseasonal blast of winter snow.

Chapter 35

The Big One

Living in New England, we get used to crazy weather. The year before we had near summer temperatures for a few days in the late fall, so it wasn't uncommon to see things out of the ordinary. However, this would be no mild snow shower that could possibly drop a dusting or an inch. It was a major storm and it was predicted to drop anywhere from 6 inches to a foot of snow.

Normally we don't even bat an eye at anything fewer than 12 inches in the north, but it was the fall and most of the trees still had leaves on them. This meant that the snow would collect in large amounts on the trees branches and cause a lot of them to bow and crack from the immense weight. This would be a huge problem as all the news channels warned since it could potentially cause power lines to come down with the falling branches.

Once again during the days leading up to the storm my wife and I stayed glued to the TV. It was just the perfect send off for my last treatment to go with all the other bad things I had been through this year. The only reason this storm would be any different than Irene was because of how cold it was going to be this time. With my sensitivity to the cold, any exposure to cold objects or even cold air could, at times, be extremely painful.

Looking for any signs of good news, we watched the weather every day hoping for a change, but with each passing day it stayed the same. Sure enough, on the last weekend of October the storm hit and hit hard. The snow started falling on Saturday, two days before the start of my last treatment, and by mid day the damage started to arise.

As the storm pounded away, trees all over the state of Connecticut gave in to the weight of the snow as it collected on the branches, taking with them power lines all over. Almost the entire state went into a blackout. The rest of the evening we watched the snow fall and once again found ourselves playing board games by candlelight. With each passing hour we grew ever more anxious for the power to return and bring us warmth and light, but it didn't. That evening we went to bed cold and disappointed. Hoping that with the coming of the next morning the power would return we slept as the snow continued to fall.

With morning light creeping through the blinds we woke and discovered the electricity was still out and there was a foot of fresh snow on the ground. Looking around outside the window we could see branches everywhere were sagging from the weight of the snow. We piled on layers of clothes to get ready for the cold day ahead. With no electricity - which meant no TV, internet, or radio - we hadn't really known the extent of the damage that the storm had left in its wake. We spent almost the entire day catching up on long neglected chores. With nothing to distract us, we busied ourselves cleaning, rearranging, and organizing things we had put off for a long time. Meanwhile, we both wondered exactly how long would we be without power. The day went on and soon evening came. Light from the sun was beginning to fade leaving us with nothing but candlelight again. It started to become obvious that due to the damage from the storm we weren't going to get our electricity back any time soon.

We woke up in the morning still without power. The cell phone tower had been knocked out during the storm, so we couldn't call to see if my treatment was still on. We were cold from having spent about 36 hours without heat and hungry because by now all of our food had spoiled. We made the decision to go to my treatment even though we didn't know what to expect. We went to my final chemo treatment the following morning; even though the power was out we were lucky enough to learn that they had a back up generator. Due to difficulties with my insurance company, my final two treatments would take place at the hospital instead of at the doctor's office. Since it was a hospital, they were set up for emergencies as blackouts and had a back-up generator. So, at least we would have heat and food for a few hours. Despite the fact that this last treatment was going to be a bit more difficult under the circumstances, I looked forward to it. It was my last one and I just wanted it to be done and over with.

I arrived with a smile on my face, eager to go. It had been six months now since I started doing chemo, and I was so excited to finally be done once and for all, hopefully. Sitting in my chair I undid the top few buttons of what had come to be known as "my chemo treatment shirt" and awaited for the nurse to plunge the needle in to my chest for what was hopefully to be the last time.

She gently cleaned the area around my implant and gathered the supplies together to get me set up. With a deep breath in and clenching my eyes shut the needle forced its way through my skin and into the implant. It hurt just as much as every other time, but by this time I had been jabbed in the chest so many times it didn't faze me as much. Now that the needle was in I once again held my breath as the nurse flushed the port in my chest with saline solution. I always held my breath because of the way the saline solution always rushed straight to the blood vessels in my nose and left me with a very unpleasant order in my nose for a moment. Sometimes holding my breath worked, other times it did nothing and I had no choice but to grin and bear it.

Everything was going smoothly for my final visit, the line to my heart that connected to my port was clean as usual, my blood count was right where it needed to be and I felt great. Since all signs pointed to green, they brought in the chemicals and hooked them up to my chest. As the treatment started I relaxed and laid back into my chair pulling up the foot rest. Although I knew the next few days would be filled with my usual misery, it meant nothing right now. I was going to be free soon.

As I sat in my chair day dreaming about my soon to come freedom, I was able to access the internet via my cell phone and discovered that almost the entire state had lost power. News stations from all over were reporting massive amounts of downed trees that had destroyed power lines. They were predicting that we could be without power for days, perhaps a week. We started to realize that we needed to do something because we couldn't stay home for days without power, especially since I was on chemo. Kellee headed out into the hall to start calling hotels to try and find us a room. We had heard that Massachusetts, which was only a few miles away, had electricity. After a few calls she found a hotel that had one room left. We immediately booked it. We were comforted by the thought that at least now we would have someplace warm to stay while we waited for the power to return to our home.

The rest of the visit went as usual, chemicals flowed into me, my wife and I talked, and we both ate a small lunch. All of the nurses I had met since this whole ordeal began stopped by my room to say hi and tell me how pleased they were to see that I was getting better. I had come a long way since the first time they met me. In the beginning I was super thin, pale white, and could barely walk due to being so weak. Now I had my full color back, I had put a few pounds back on, and I was full of energy.

With the in-office treatment coming to an end, my trusty little pump was hooked up to me and we were sent on our way. We drove home and started packing our suitcases for the next few days. Both of us packed as many warm clothes as we could just incase something happened while we were at the hotel. With all our necessities packed up, we hopped in the car and headed north into Massachusetts to our temporary home away from home.

Arriving at the hotel a short while later, we grabbed a luggage cart and headed inside to check in. Looking around it was very apparent that most of the people there had the same idea as us to stay at a hotel in order to stay warm. We ended up being very fortunate to get the last room. I don't think one hotel in the area ended up with a single free room. Thankfully, this was a nice hotel and not some dive that we would have to worry about it being clean.

Had there not been a room available we could have stayed at my wife's parent's house. Although they had lost electricity as well, they had a wood burning stove that would have kept me warm which was our main concern. However, their driveway had been blocked off by a fallen tree and to get to the house we would have had to hike up the snow-covered long steep driveway with our bags. Staying at a hotel was the most convenient option. Plus we didn't want to burden them with worrying about caring for me.

We checked in and headed to our room to get settled. It was nice to be someplace that had both heat and electricity. It was starting to look like this might not be such a bad experience. It was almost like a mini vacation without the hassles of traveling to some far-off destination. Content with our decision, we brought our bags into the room and started to make ourselves at home.

Chapter 36

Home Away From Home

Kellee and I had stayed in hotels a million times in the past, but this would be by far one of the most memorable stays we had encountered. It was destined to be one of those stories you tell for many years. It wasn't exactly a fond memory, but a memory of a small hurdle in life that we overcame.

Since I was undergoing my treatment, I had no desire to set foot out of the room unless I had to. I spent almost all of my time lying on the bed watching TV to keep my mind off of the situation. I came to find out early on that watching movies, playing video games, or watching television shows were the perfect distraction. No matter what I always felt sick to my stomach, weak, and achy from head to toe. Watching mindless entertainment helped me keep my mind off things so that even for a short while I could forget everything I was going through and escape.

Nights were the most difficult time for me while undergoing treatment. Every time I would start a new treatment, the evening of the first day the muscles in my lower half of my legs would ache uncontrollably. I would load up on pain killers before bed to ease my legs muscles. Then I would spend the rest of the night drifting in and out of sleep with my head feeling fuzzy from the meds. Now I had to do this in unfamiliar surroundings and remind myself every time I woke up where I was.

The most difficult part of any night while doing treatments was dealing with the pump. The first few times I had ever done it I was so paranoid I would not move a muscle all night. I would lie on my back with pillows propped under my legs to help keep me from moving and do my best to stay in one position.

By now though, I had gotten used to the pump and spent most nights more relaxed and sleeping in different positions. I still had to be very cautious and conscious of it all night long, but I had worked out a system to keep me from any harm. I always kept the pump close to my body away from my wife, and I always kept the strap close to my hand and several times a night I would check to make sure I hadn't pinched off the line. Had I pinched the line an alarm would have gone off to warn me, but being the paranoid person I am, I always checked it anyway.

That first night in the hotel it was business as usual. I kept the pump close to me and would wake constantly to make sure no harm came to it, or me. Even though I had done this many times before I was still a bit more paranoid since I was in unfamiliar surroundings. Being in a different bed, there's always the fear of rolling too close to the edge and dropping the pump, or who knows what. I did what I could to try and rest but most of the night was spent tossing and turning as usual.

The following morning with no problems or casualties, we readied ourselves to go have breakfast in the lobby. One of the perks of the hotel was a free all you can eat breakfast every morning. As good as that may sound, for me it wasn't all good news, I was feeling sick and nauseous from the chemotherapy so I had to be careful of what, and how much I ate.

As we walked down the hall towards the lobby I started to get a little nervous. I have always been a self-conscious person and never really cared about being the center of attention. And now I was going to be that guy you see who has some type of medical device hooked up to him that everyone stares at. I tried my best to keep it concealed as I put food on my plate but I could already feel eyes from around the room falling upon me. As I headed to a table to sit I took quick glances around the room and sure enough people were staring, trying to figure out what the machine was that I was hooked up to. Little kids of course are the worst offenders, being young and naive they don't know any better and natural curiosity takes over and they just stare uncontrollably.

Trying my best to ignore them, I kept my head down as I ate and just stared at my food. I guess in a sense I was a bit more fortunate than other cancer fighters, I had not lost my hair like some do, so to most people I looked totally normal with the exception of the pump hanging from my shoulder.

It was for reasons like being stared at that I never left my home while being treated, the only exception was to have the pump removed and to bring Kellee to the hospital when she broke her vertebrae. I didn't like anyone seeing me with it, not even my friends and family. The biggest reason for hiding it from strangers is the "freak factor". People see it and look at you and think to themselves, "What is wrong with him? Why does he have that thing? Is he sick? Is he contagious?" You can see the look on their face and know thoughts like that or similar are going through their heads and it makes you feel like a freak, an outcast.

Kellee and I chatted about the day ahead as we ate which helped distract me from the staring eyes. Another quick glance around the room revealed most of the people had stopped looking at me, but a few lingered. I made a small mention to my wife about the situation and told her it was making me uncomfortable. She told me it was alright and to just ignore them, as she patted my hand.

My wife Kellee is the total opposite of me; she loves attention, loves being in the spotlight and is just an all around ham. She knows that I for the most part want nothing to do with the spotlight, so she is usually sympathetic to my needs in the matter. She continued to talk about other things to keep me from thinking about the people around us.

A few minutes later we finished our breakfast and headed back to the room. I could feel my stress levels drop once we were inside. Kellee had some errands to take care of and left me in the room while she ran around town tying up loose ends. I spent the day as usual sitting around watching TV waiting for time to pass. She returned later that afternoon and told me that power had been restored back in our town.

It was a miracle, our town is out in the middle of nowhere and is usually last to get things fixed when it comes to situations like this, but somehow it was back. Knowing our luck and that just because it was back right now, didn't mean it would stay, we decided to stay one more night at the hotel like we had planned and wait to see what happens.

That night was much like the last. I rolled around constantly trying to find a comfortable position to lie in while trying to keep the pump safe. Nights with the pump aren't just troublesome for me; my constant stirring usually disturbs my wife and prevents her from sleeping too. I feel awful about it and apologize often about it, but it's out of my control. She understands that, so she usually doesn't get too mad at me. We just both get out of bed the next morning cranky and tired, dreading the day to come.

The following morning we packed our bags and got ready to leave. We had planned to just put everything in the car and go straight to the doctor's office rather than drop our stuff off at home. This way I could get the pump off sooner and I could be of more help when we unpacked the car later.

I wouldn't be surprised if I had a smile on my face the whole way to the doctor's office. I felt sick, I was cold, I was tired, but I was excited. It was a huge milestone in my life, my chemotherapy was finally coming to an end - this was it. It was finally over! It had all seemed like one big, long bad dream, and now I was about to wake from it.

We entered the office both of us smiling and anxious barely able to hide our excitement. I paced back and forth in the lobby waiting to be called into the back and say goodbye to PIA. The little pump had helped save my life, but it definitely lived up to the name Pain in the Ass or PIA as we called her. It was certainly a love hate relationship, with more hate than love, but it was soon to be over.

One of the nurses poked her head down the hall and called me to the back. She knew it was my last time too, so she also had a big smile on her face. Kellee and I rushed to the back. I plopped myself down into the chair and awaited my freedom. Once they finished with the other patients it was my turn. Still smiling, they asked me how I was doing and my only reply was "I am great."

With the last few drops leaving the pump and entering me for the last time, they closed off the lines and started to disconnect me. They flushed my port with saline and the anticoagulant one last time then began to peel back the tape that held the needle in my chest. Once off they did a final three, two, one countdown and pulled the needle out of my chest and bandaged me up.

I was sore from the tape and the needle but I could care less. The end that we never thought would come was here. It was over, I was free, and I was happy. We made an appointment for a follow up visit in 3 weeks to check on me and to schedule a CAT scan to see if the treatments were a success. Saying goodbye we left and drove home. I stared out the window at the snow thinking to myself just how beautiful it was and how great life was at that moment.

Although I still had more doctor visits to do before it would all be truly over, this part that had been such a huge burden in my life had come to pass. A huge weight had been lifted off my shoulders and all I could do was smile. I was happy and content for the first time in a long time.

We wouldn't know the final results for several weeks until a CAT scan was done, but I was confident. As far as I was concerned I won - I had beaten cancer. Against all of the odds, I had overcome this horrible disease and would live on to talk about it. I finally almost had my life back.

Chapter 37

Dinner With A Side Of Hit And Run

For many months Kellee and I had discussed celebrating the end of my treatments. We bounced back and forth on where to go and what to do before finally deciding on going out to eat at one of our favorite restaurants. We chose this particular place because it held a lot of sentimental value to us and her family. Her parents had been going there for several years and were acquaintances with the owners and their family. They took me there a few times and during one of the times my parents came up from Virginia to visit us we all went to dinner there to celebrate our engagement.

They have excellent food, a nice atmosphere, and we always have a good time when we are there. So, it was chosen to be our place of celebration. We made our reservations and planned our whole night out together. We would head out early evening, have a nice leisurely dinner, relax, talk, and just enjoy ourselves.

When the day finally came we got dressed up in nice clothes. I wore khakis pants and a nice sweater. She wore dress slacks and a sweater as well. A splash of cologne, a spray of perfume, and we were ready for a night on the town. We had been looking forward to this night for months. It had been so long since we enjoyed a nice time out. Other than our vacation we had spent every night for the last 6 months home.

It's just a short drive to the restaurant. We arrived in no time, parked, and headed in. We planned to take our time throughout the night and not rush the meal. We just wanted to sit and enjoy ourselves and our food, something we had been missing for some time. It would be something I would enjoy even more since I no longer had to deal with the nausea from the chemotherapy. I was free to enjoy every bite and every sip.

As the night went on we did just as we had planned. We had a cheese sampler plate for our appetizer. We sipped our drinks as we nibbled and awaited our dinner. We talked about how nice it was to be out of the house someplace nice instead of a doctor's office. We discussed future plans, and places we wanted to go, and things we wanted to do.

Neither one of us had been this relaxed in almost a year. The warm comforting surroundings just wrapped pleasant thoughts around us and melted away our stress. It was a welcomed change from what had become the norm for us. Chemo was finally over, I was feeling great, and as far as we knew everything had been a success.

After dinner we sat and continued to sip on our drinks and talk the night away. Just like everything else, it had been a long time since we had really sat and talked like that. We began to reconnect with one another and remember just how much we enjoyed one another's company. I was no longer sick, she no longer had to care for me and worry about me. It had both of us floating.

Feeling full and content we put our coats on and headed for the exit, we said goodbye to our waiter and the host and made our way for the door. Once outside I noticed some selfish fool had made his own parking space and was now blocking more than half of the walkway to the front door, which was also a wheelchair access ramp. In disbelief that someone could be so stupid and uncaring, we both shook our heads as we passed by. We walked across the small parking lot which is just big enough to fit a row of cars on each side and a gap big enough for one car to drive by at a time.

Reaching my car I unlocked it and stopped dead in my tracks. A car was headed through the parking lot and headed for one of the exits which was next to my car. I only noticed the car because it was driving very close to the parked cars on the opposite side of where I was parked. As he crept closer to my wife and me, I noticed that when the person had made their own parking place it caused the back end of their SUV to stick out very far compared to the rest of the cars. The approaching car was going to have to fit between my car and the SUV.

Before I could even react, it was too late. The driver had hit the back corner of the bumper on the SUV with a loud thud. To my surprise the driver didn't get out to inspect the damage, instead to my absolute shock the driver stepped on the gas. Hitting the bumper had stopped him and now he was forcing his car to push against the SUV to get by it. The SUV rocked slightly as the side of the car scraped along the bumper. Creaking, cracking and scraping its way by as the whole side of the car slid across the SUV's bumper. Once again I expected the driver to stop and realize what he had done and own up to his mistake. Judging from his actions thus far it was very possible that the person had drunk too much alcohol that night. Kellee and I waited to see if the driver would get out and what his reaction would be, but once he cleared past the SUV he hit the gas and took off for the exit. I couldn't believe what I had just seen.

With out time to think I ran toward the car and memorized his license plate number. I read it and repeated it over and over again in my head. Looking back at my wife her mouth was ajar; she was in as much disbelief as I was. I told her I memorized his plate number and that we should head inside and report him.

Back inside we found the host and began to tell him what we had just witnessed; he stopped me mid sentence and asked if the SUV blocking the walkway was hit. Surprised and thinking he had seen it too I said yes. He just shook his head and mumbled something to the effect of only an idiot would park there as he followed us outside. Walking around to the back of the SUV we saw the carnage left behind by the other driver.

There were deep gashes in the bumper scraped all the way down to the plastic, on the ground lay broken trim pieces from the molding on the other car that gave way to the stress of the impact. Again the host shook his head and asked himself out loud, "What kind of idiot parks here? It's their fault. This isn't a parking space."

With one final look at the damage we headed back inside, I told him the plate number and the general direction the driver headed in. He wrote it down and continued to shake his head while trying to fathom what goes through peoples minds when they do things like this. After we gave our statement we tried once again to leave and head for home.

Back out in the parking lot we looked once more at the damage and headed over to my car. Opening my car door I noticed another car headed our way taking the exact same path as the other one. Realizing my car might be hit this time, I jumped in, started it and turned on the lights to let the person know I was there.

At first they paused to see if I was going to pull out, but I couldn't move because Kellee was standing outside the car with the door open watching the person, icy stare and hands on hips non-verbally saying, " Go ahead, hit our car, and then we'll see what I do to you." The car started moving again causing fears of my car being hit next to race through my mind. I tried desperately to get Kellee's attention to tell her to get in the car so I could move out of the way.

With mere seconds to spare, she finally realized I was trying to get her in the car, hopped in and closed the door. As the door was closing, I threw my car in reverse to move it back just in time for the car to miss slamming into me. Had I been a few seconds slower the other car would have hit the front of my car for sure. Once the car had passed we pulled out and left as fast as possible before the next car came along. We couldn't believe people could be so careless like that, then not own up to their mistakes. It not only affects their lives, but the lives of those whose property they damage.

It's moments like this that make me question humanity as a whole, and to this day I still wonder what happened to the driver who hit the other car. I can only hope he got what he deserved.

Chapter 38

Down To The Last Minute

Three weeks later I had my next doctor visit. I was looked over from head to toe and asked how I was doing. The truth was that I was doing fantastic. I felt great, better than I had in years. My only complaint was that my hands and feet were still numb, and as I was told, would be numb for several weeks to months until the nerves healed.

While there, we discussed my condition and my future. Now that chemo was over I had to schedule a CAT scan to have a look inside me and search for any traces of cancer. If it came up clear it meant that it had all been worth it and I had won. If there were any signs at all that cancer cells remained then future treatments would have to be discussed.

After leaving the doctor's office, I stopped by the surgeon's office to schedule an appointment for a consultation prior to having my port removed. The nurse there was happy to see me and extremely glad to see that I was doing so well. I told her the good news and what was planned and she penciled me in.

A few weeks later I had my visit with the surgeon and he too was very glad to see that I was doing so well. I thanked him again for everything that he had done for me. If it wasn't for his skilled hands and knowledge, I wouldn't be alive today. Being the humble man that he is, he always tells me that seeing me healthy is his reward.

We talked over what the procedure would entail and as long as I was in good health, it would be a go. We scheduled the CAT scan for one week before the surgery to give the doctors plenty of time to look over the results, or so we thought.

When the time came for the CAT scan I once again had to starve myself and drink the nasty tasting dye. You're supposed to mix it with a drink of your choice to help make it more tolerable, but all it does is make whatever you put it in taste rancid. Reluctantly I drank it, complaining with each swig as I shuddered at the horrid taste.

A short while later I was at the hospital waiting for my scan, starving and watching the morning news in the lobby when the tech finally came to get me. She introduced herself and asked me if I had ever done a CAT scan before to which I replied, "Oh yeah!" Guessing I had done it more than once she asked me how many times, I told her about 3-4 so far which made her stop in her tracks and ask me if it was all in one year. I told her it was and she politely asked me what was wrong with me. I somewhat smirked when I told her. The reason I smirked is because I knew the response I would get once I informed her of my condition. Sure enough when I told her I had colon cancer she again stopped walking and said what they all say "Oh my god, you're too young for that." If only it were true.

After a quick change into another set of lovely hospital gowns I was on the table being injected with more dye. Ten minutes later and a quick scan of my insides and I was free to go. Wishing me luck, the tech said goodbye and I headed home. The next week would be filled with nothing but anxiety as we waited for the results from the scan.

Was it all worth it? Did it work? Did I beat cancer? Will I go on living? As sure as I was that all the answers to those questions were yes, a sliver of doubt always loomed over me. It's human nature to expect the worst, and in my case, I usually got it. This time I was fairly confident that things would be different.

It was now Wednesday and I still had not heard from my doctor. The scan had been done on Monday and figured they would have gotten the results by now. I called my oncologist's office to ask if they had gotten them yet to which they replied no. With no other choice, I had to wait a few more days.

Friday came and I still had not gotten a call, so mid-afternoon I called again and they still could not find them. Getting nervous I called my surgeon's office to see if they had gotten the results yet. It turned out that they did, but the surgeon had not looked at them yet. Since none of my doctors would be available over the weekend, I told the receptionist on the phone that it was very important he review them. It was Friday afternoon and I was scheduled for surgery on Monday. We needed to know the results as soon as possible otherwise we would have to cancel the whole thing.

As the day wound down on Friday I never got the call from either office. What was I supposed to do now? My surgery was still scheduled and I didn't want to cancel it unless we knew for sure that I still had cancer. With no other choice, we decided to wait the weekend out and hope for a phone call first thing Monday morning before we headed to the hospital.

Early Monday morning came and went without a phone call. The time came for us to leave for the hospital. So, we figured we would just go and tell the nurses about the scan results and have someone track them down. We arrived at the hospital and went in to the same day surgery department as usual. I was once again greeted by all the nurses that my wife and I had come to know and like. We were greeted with warm smiles and congratulations on my continued success. After we said our hellos, we explained to them what we had been going through all week with trying to track down my CAT scan results and asked them for help. They told us they would take care of it and for us not to worry. We were led into my pre-op room and I was asked one more time to slip into yet another hospital gown.

One of the worst parts about going into surgery, other than the procedure itself, is the wait time. They have you come in two hours early, sometimes more, just to sit and wait for your turn to go in. This time was no different. We waited for two hours agonizing over what the results of my scan were and if we were wasting our time or not. I was more nervous this time about getting the results than the actual surgery. I was actually looking forward to the surgery, if it was going to happen.

Before we knew it the nurse came to take me to operating room waiting area. Upon entering the room he saw me and with a big smile on his face said "Oh no, not you again, you're back," To which I retorted with "I know, we really do need to stop meeting like this." Every time I went in for any of my procedures, he was the person pushing me from room to room on the bed and just like everyone else he always told me I was too young for all this.

The wheels on my bed were unlocked and I was on my way to the waiting area, my wife accompanied me and was allowed to stay with me until it was time to go in. I was now minutes away from surgery and still had no word if anyone had looked at my chart. We once again had to ask someone if the surgeon had seen the chart and finally right down to the last minute it was finally in his hands. We were told he had them and was reviewing them now, talk about a sigh of relief. Finally we would get some answers.

While we waited there was a woman in the bed next to me. The curtain was closed but we could overhear her talking to a nurse about her upcoming colonoscopy and how she was worried because last time they found a small bump of some sort. Upon hearing this, my wife and I looked at one another and rolled our eyes as we thought about all that I had been through in the last year. She had every reason to be worried, but still, compared to what I had just been through it seemed so trivial to us.

Lying in my bed I did my best to keep myself calm. I was slightly nervous, but more anxious than anything. My wife held my hand and talked with me. Neither one of us could believe how close we were cutting this. For all we knew I could be told bad news and taken back to my room and all this waiting would have been for nothing.

Finally, after an eternity of waiting, the surgeon came around the corner, grinning from ear to ear he said hello and told us the news we had been waiting on edge to hear. The scan came up clean, there were no visible traces left in my abdomen and the surgery was a go. It was the best news I had received in my entire life (Well, except for when Kellee said she would marry me).

I had beaten the odds and overcome an illness that claims so many. All the suffering I had endured was worth it. My cancer was under control and I had a new lease on life. I told the surgeon it was great news worth waiting for. We explained to him what we had just been through trying to get the results and he told us that I should have just called his office. I told him I called on Friday and told the receptionist on the phone the importance of it and to get it to him right away. Hearing this he got an angry look on his face and apologized. It turned out the receptionist never gave him the message.

Now we had our answers and it was time to have the port removed. I said goodbye to my wife as I was wheeled into the operating room. Inside everyone remembered me from when I had the port first implanted. Just like everyone else they were happy to see me and thrilled with my progress.

By this time I knew the routine. They wheeled me over to the operating table and had me crawl on to it and lay down so they could begin the prep work. My lower half was wrapped in heated blankets while they pulled down the top of my gown to reveal my chest. As they got me ready they went over the procedure with me once again and explained just like last time I would be awake during the whole thing, and only given a general pain killer through the I.V. and a local anesthetic.

Ready to go and eager to have it out, the procedure was about to begin. I felt the sharp painful pricks from the needle in my chest as the local anesthetic as administered. I was injected several times in a circle around the port to be sure the whole area would be numb. Just as the general pain killer was hitting my body the doctor went to make the first incision. Suddenly I felt the scalpel cutting into my chest and let out a quick shriek of pain. The surgeon stopped instantly and asked me if I had felt that. I told him I did and they once again stuck me with more needles to inject more anesthesia in me as well as push more painkillers in through my I.V.

Confident I was good to go; he went on with the procedure. This time I felt nothing. The medicine was now working and I just laid there and waited. I was starting to feel very relaxed from the pain killers and found myself staring at the lights through the blue paper they placed over my face to keep me from seeing what they were doing. About ten minutes later, they pulled the paper from my face and unstrapped me. I slid back over onto my bed and was on my way to the recovery room.

Just like before, they kept me in the recovery room for about twenty minutes to monitor me and be sure I was okay before sending me back to my room. After the short wait I was pushed back to my room only to find out there was another patient and his family in there. In all the times I had been in the hospital before I always had my own room. I was a little confused by the presence of these other people since my wife was not in there waiting for me. To my relief once they locked my bed in place she entered the room and joined me by my side.

She told me that when I went into the operating room she came back to find them in the room, so she went to wait for me in the waiting room. I didn't mind that they were there since I was only going to be here for another half hour or so. In the end they turned out to not be in the room for very long, he was on his way into surgery as I was on my way out.

Feeling good, minus the sore spot in my chest, I was once again very happy. I no longer had to deal with the hard lump in my chest or be weary of people bumping it or hugging me too tight. The little invader was gone. It was yet another step to my life returning back to normal. Slowly but surely, piece by piece I was getting my life back.

Chapter 39

It's A Wonderful Life

After my surgery I would be spending the rest of the week at home recovering and doped up on pain killers. I could get around alright and for the most part function normally, but simple things like getting dressed were not easy tasks. I had a lot of trouble with the mobility of my left arm and could barely lift it up over my head to put a shirt on with out being in pain. I was more fortunate this time around since I remembered how to work around this issue when I had the implant first put in. It was still painful but it made the task faster and easier on me.

Since I was once again going to be stuck at home for awhile I found myself just like before, trying to find things to keep myself occupied. My usual routine consisted of lining up movies and TV shows for each day. However this time around a special surprise was in store for me, one that was both expected and unexpected, Santa was going to pay me a visit.

Every year I take part in a Secret Santa event with the crowd on the BMW website Bimmer Forums that I mentioned earlier. All the participants are matched with other people and we buy each other gifts and send them out. No one knows who their Santa (gift giver) is until the gift arrives and they reveal themselves.

It's something that I enjoy and look forward to all year long. It's usually good for a laugh and a few surprises, but this year I was in store for something absolutely amazing. It was coming down to the deadline of Christmas Eve and with just a few days to go I still had not received my gift(s) from my Secret Santa. Since time was running out, I was starting to wonder if I was "dead-beated," which is when someone does not follow through and send out a gift like they are supposed to.

As it just so happened on the very day of my surgery none the less, my wife and I arrive home and start to settle in. A short while later I get a call from Kellee's mother telling me that two very large packages arrived for me and were waiting for me at work. I asked her if they were to me personally and she asked if I also went by a second name (which happened to be my user name on the BMW website) that was printed on the box. I told her that was me and that I would be right down to get them.

I told my wife they had arrived and that we had to get them right away, of course I only had one good arm so I would need her help. Moments later I had my shoes back on and out the door we went. When I arrived at work, I could not believe how large the boxes were. I started to get really excited just like a little kid on Christmas morning. With the help of my wife we each took one of the boxes and lugged them back home.

Once we finally managed to get them up the stairs and into our home, I grabbed my utility knife and cut them open. Inside, amongst the packing peanuts, I could see faint glimpses of bright red wrapping paper. It had a slight shimmer to it and just begged to be ripped open.

I reached in and grabbed package after package from each box along with a few mysterious looking large manila envelopes and one small white envelope. By the time I was done I had two large piles of presents waiting to be opened. There must have been somewhere near two dozen gifts ranging from small little packages to a few large ones. Normally a person receives a just a few gifts. We set a twenty dollar minimum with no cap on how much you can spend, but on average most people spend around forty dollars and get someone a few nice or funny gifts.

Whoever my Santa was this year went all out and really spoiled me. I sat on the floor just looking at them all in complete disbelief. Guessing that the small white envelope had a card in it with the gift givers name, I opened that first. I read the card then started to laugh when I got to the name. It was from my friend Sachin. He was the same person who sent me the gifts when my mother died and he was also the person who organized the Secret Santa gig. It looked like he had saved me to be his victim this year and boy was I right.

The large envelopes were all labeled with letters. There was envelope "A" and "B" and one that read "Mission Statement" and finally one that was labeled "Open first". All I could do was sit and laugh and wonder at what on earth this crazy man was up to. I opened the envelope labeled "Open First" and discovered that he had put together a whole elaborate theme for my gifts.

It's no secret to anyone that I am a huge Batman fan. I collect many items from toys to models to clothes and everything in between. I had mentioned at one point in the past on the BMW website that I was having a lot of issues with my insurance company covering my medical bills. Well Sachin put together a whole array of Batman themed "gear" to aide me in a mission to seek revenge on them for stiffing me with the bills.

Upon opening the presents I found everything from a disguise to hide my identity to toy weapons to help fight the bad guys with. Sachin had really outdone himself this year and proven just how wonderful of a friend he truly is. With Kellee's help we took photos of all the gifts and the letters to show to everyone on the website. Sure enough everyone got a huge kick out of it and gave well deserving praises to Sachin for his idea. Everyone loved the outstanding effort he put into making sure that after the horrible year I had experienced. I could at least have a wonderful Christmas.

That week was full of a lot of good news, I had beaten cancer and was given a clean bill of health, and I also had the best Christmas that I could remember since I was a child. It was nice to finally have some joy in my life after all the horrible things that my family and I had been through. For once there was a shinning light at the end of the dark tunnel, finally something good worth remembering.

Chapter 40

It's Over. Or Is It?

Shortly after Christmas, the year had finally come to an end. It had been a year filled with pain and anger, death and depression. On New Year's Eve my wife and I opened a bottle of champagne. I poured a glass for each of us and held mine up. Kellee followed my lead and asked me what we should toast to. I thought about it for a moment, remembering all we had been through, and then I moved my glass towards hers and said "Here is to a new year and putting all this behind us. Let the next year be filled with happiness and less pain, and no more bad news." We clanked our glasses together and each took a sip.

Though the year was over and I had overcome my illness, the effect that it had on both of our lives would change us forever. Life would never be the same for my wife and I or anyone in our family for that matter. The loss of my mother had a huge impact on my father, my brothers, and I. The woman who all during our childhood was the most important woman on earth to us and meant so much to us into adulthood was gone. My father lost the love of his life, the woman who was the world to him. That was something that could never be fixed.

At the same time that I was beginning my battle, the world lost a hero when my grandfather passed on. I came very close to dying myself shortly after that, but in the end I survived my battle while my mother and grandfather did not. Two very loved members of my family were gone, pushing my family's compassion and sanity to its limits. Experiencing what my family had been through was enough to drive any one person, even a whole family, to the proverbial edge. It took a lot of strength to deal with all that we had been through and not give up on the world and life itself.

We pulled together when it was most important and provided the love and strength that was needed for us to persevere. There is a lot that can be said about the power of love. It can make one accomplish the greatest of feats and endure the toughest of times. Without the love and support of my wife, my family, and my friends, I think it is safe to say that I would not be here today.

I know I am lucky in the fact that I had so much support from everyone, and all they contributed to helping give me a positive attitude and outlook on my life. I know that not everyone has that luxury, but in all honesty, even if I just had one person in my life to look to, it would have been enough. I learned early on that I was not going to face this battle alone. As I have discovered through my own experiences, no one has to face this, or any illness alone. Much to my surprise, I learned that compassion still exists in the hearts of strangers, and people that you have never met before are more than willing to help another in need.

I used to believe that mankind had given up on itself, and that the desire to help others no longer mattered to anyone anymore. The kindness that total strangers showed me when I came forth about my illness made me realize that I was wrong. Upon learning of my suffering, people who lived clear across the country, even the world, stepped forward and offered me help in any way they could. All I ever asked for from them was that they keep positive thoughts of me in their mind and in turn, help to try and keep me positive. While it was nice to know that if I really needed help for anything else that they would be there, all I really wanted was someone to listen and wish me well.

To this day and for the rest of my life, I will forever believe that one of the biggest contributors to my beating this illness was my positive attitude. I knew that if I kept my head up and pushed on no matter what got in my way I would beat it. As I have mentioned before, I have lived by the philosophy that no matter what bad things may come in life, there are always things to be grateful for.

My own faith was pushed to its limits during this period of my life.

Almost everything in my life that was good was taken away from me and I struggled day to day to reclaim some of it back. There were times when I almost lost hope and I came very close to wanting to just give up. Every time I thought things could not get any worse they did, it seemed like the world was coming to an end and everything I held dear was being taken from me.

I never gave up though. I was pushed to my limits and beyond but I held strong. I know because of this I have become a much stronger person than I already was, and I know that if I ever need more than I can give, others will be there to help pick me back up. I will never have to face my battles alone.

Not everyone wins their battle with cancer like I did. A lot of people in this world fight harder than I ever could imagine and still lose their battles. A dear friend of mine named Jesse is one of those people fighting an ever increasing battle, fighting for her life with each passing day. Before I wrote my book I never knew that she existed. I had no idea of just what she had been going through the last few years that eventually made our paths in life cross one another. Fate had once again stepped into my life, only this time it was for something good.

Another member on the car forum that I frequent started a thread one day talking about a close friend of his named Jesse. The main topic of the thread was about a new experimental approach to fighting cancer and how his friend was going to apply for it in hopes of finally being able to get control of her life back. Jay told us briefly about his friend and asked us all to keep her in our thoughts. Little did he know the implications that would result from this.

Before he knew it the forum exploded with post after post all wishing her well, and along with that, offers came flooding in to help her and send her gifts. Once again we all banded together and did everything we could in our power to give her strength and courage to fight on. Much like they did with me, the other members jumped in and encouraged her to keep on fighting. One after another offered words of comfort to inspire her and lift her spirits. We shared stories of our own, asked her a lot of questions to get to know her and in no time we all learned just how amazing this young woman really was.

As time went on, we found out that she loved traveling but because of her illness she had not been able to go anywhere for some time. Hoping to lift her spirits, the members started posting up pictures from all over the world of them holding signs saying "Hi Jess". Since she couldn't travel, we traveled for her and took her with us in spirit.

Just as we had hoped, it brought a smile to her face and helped her realize there was a lot more worth fighting for than she had known. She had discovered what I had the year before. No one is ever truly alone. You never have to face such horrible situations like these by yourself. If you need help, just ask. If you're afraid, don't be. Just tell your story and you will realize just how willing people are to jump in and help you, even if they are complete strangers.

When I compare my own battle with cancer to hers, I had it easy. As difficult as it was for me to experience the things I went through, this poor girl has suffered a million times worse. Yet despite that she never gave in. She held on and fought with everything she had. She refused to give up and succumb to this horrible illness. She showed more strength and resilience than anyone I had ever met in my entire life.

After having been through this and knowing what it's like, my heart goes out to people like her and those closest to them. No one should ever have to experience the kind of suffering that comes with such a disease. My wife often wondered if we would have been better off if it had been her that had been sick and me that took care of her. My only reply to that has been I wish this disease on no one. No person should ever have to go through this and I am glad it was me and not her. Knowing what it was like, I could never watch her suffer and go through the things that I experienced.

Though I have won this battle, my war will go on forever. Due to the exact nature of my disease, it is very likely that I will be battling cancer for the rest of my life. The genetic mutation that exists in my DNA will forever plague me and make me highly susceptible to getting cancer over and over again.

It pains me to say it, think it, and accept it, but given what is known about the specifics of my condition, the survival rate isn't the best. I was diagnosed with stage III colon cancer which means that the cancer spread from my colon to the inner wall of my abdomen and into some lymph nodes. I have basically been told by every doctor that I will be very lucky to reach old age since stage III cancer usually only gives about a 63% survival rate past 5 years. I am thirty years old now, reaching the age of forty seems probable, I will be lucky to reach fifty, and beyond that who knows.

I might be one of those one in a million cases where it goes into remission and never returns or I may have several battles ahead of me, each one taking years away from my life. It's a hard fact to swallow knowing there is a very good chance I will never reach old age. I may never get to enjoy my golden years and look back on a long lived accomplished life. It's difficult for anyone to know their own mortality and be aware of the fact that their life will be cut short.

I am grateful for the years that I have lived, and I know there are many children who fight cancer and lose and never get a chance to even live as long as I have. It breaks my heart knowing this, and as much as I feel cheated by my own potential short life I know they and their parents would have given anything to have the time that I have had.

Despite all that I have been through I know that I am extremely lucky to be alive and because of this I will live my life the best that I can and do my best to enjoy every moment of it. I've been given a second chance and I refuse to waste it. Other obstacles will come my way, and one day I won't be able to overcome them, but until that day comes, I refuse to give up. I will fight with everything I have for as long as I have and do what it takes to remain here alive, as long as possible.

I promised my wife that I will always be here for her. I promised that I will always be there to take care of her and love her. That is a promise I will do everything within my power to keep. I am here today because of her and I owe her my life. She stood by me day in and day out and took care of me when I needed it the most. I fought to live for her and I will fight to live for her with every ounce of strength I have for many years to come.

I have a new appreciation for life and everything and everyone in it. I look at the world around me with new born eyes and I see the beauty that was lost to me long ago. I have been through the toughest times of my life to date and have come out stronger because of it. I learned more about who I am this year than I had ever known in the past. I was pushed to my limits and survived. I am alive.

Printed in Great Britain
by Amazon